ALMOST HOME

ALMOST HOME

G. EDWARD REID

REVIEW AND HERALD® PUBLISHING ASSOCIATION
HAGERSTOWN, MD 21740

This book was
Edited by Raymond H. Woolsey
Copyedited by Jocelyn Fay and James Cavil
Designed by Trent Truman
Cover art by SquareOne Design
Typeset: 11/13 Times

PRINTED IN U.S.A.
04 03 02 01 00   5 4 3 2 1

R&H Cataloging Service
    Reid, George Edward
        Almost home

            1. Eschatoglogy. 2. Second Advent. I. Title
                            236

ISBN 0-8280-1513-9

CONTENTS

CHAPTER ONE

WHICH WAY HOME?

A number of years ago my family and I lived in Jackson, Mississippi. Early one morning I received a call from a nurse who was a member of our church. She was at work at the hospital, and she explained that they needed a chaplain to minister to a grieving family. Upon arriving at the hospital, I learned that there had been a terrible traffic accident on Interstate 55 just north of town in the wee hours of the morning. A family of five had been returning home in their station wagon from a vacation on the Gulf Coast. Likely mom and dad were up front, trying to keep each other awake as they headed back home to school and work. The three children, two boys and a girl, were sleeping. One was probably in the second seat and the other two in the back part of the station wagon.

Then something very unexpected happened. A man who had been traveling south on the same highway had stopped to rest or get gas. Perhaps confused by fatigue or alcohol, when he reentered the interstate he began driving south on the northbound lanes, right past the "Wrong Way" signs.

Just a few minutes later the station wagon with the family and the car with the lone driver met at interstate speeds in a head-on collision. Four people were killed instantly—the lone driver, and the husband and wife and one child in the other car. The two children who survived, a boy and the girl, were seriously injured and knocked unconscious. They were taken to the hospital for treatment, and as they were waking up, the hospital staff called me to explain to them what had happened—that the accident had proved fatal to their mom, dad, and brother.

It was an experience that I shall never forget. Four lives snuffed out because one person had gone the wrong way.

What could have been done to avoid the fatal crash? The most sensible thing, of course, would have been for both drivers to stop and rest when they got sleepy. But suppose that you had been in a position to warn one of the drivers of the serious consequences that were likely to occur under the circumstances. What if you had been traveling south on that interstate that night and looked across the median and seen a car traveling the same direction you were? What if you had had a CB radio and made a call, or flashed your lights, or sounded your horn, or done something else to alert the other driver of the potential danger?

What do you think the response would have been by the other driver? Maybe he or she would have said about you, "What is that crazy guy doing on the other side of the road? Must be high on something." But on the other hand, maybe the driver would have understood your warning and said, "Wow, I am going the wrong way. I must quickly change directions." Under these circumstances, would it be bigotry or an act of self-righteousness on your part to give a warning of danger? Obviously not. But today many of life's travelers are going in the wrong direction, with potentially eternal consequences. Society is plagued with such a penchant for "political correctness" and extreme tolerance that it is considered bigotry and self-righteousness to give a warning of the danger ahead!

The words "almost home" evoke feelings of anticipation and excitement. There are many songs, poems, and books written about home. "Be it ever so humble, there's no place like home." We all have roads we become very familiar with—the road from home to college and back; the road to Grandma's for Thanksgiving; the road back and forth to work. But our final—eternal—home is a place that we have only read and heard about. The location and time of arrival are quite a mystery to many people. We have never been there and must rely on outside help to make sure we are on the right road.

No problem, you say; I'll just get the directions and go. But there is a major problem. In the grand scheme of things the evil one has taken as one of his major goals to distract, sidetrack, and deceive those heading to the heavenly home. He has even prepared authentic-looking maps and guides. Though appearing to be genuine, these dispense information that will lead the traveler away from the right road. Accordingly, we must be vigilant and awake to maintain the proper focus.

The direction our life's pathway takes is largely up to us. It is based on the decisions—choices—that we make. Some of these choices may seem small and insignificant when we make them, yet many decisions made early in life have far-reaching consequences. Such decisions include whether to go to college; whether to wait to get married until both parties are mature adults with adequate education and established vocations; whether to drink alcohol, smoke, or use drugs; whether to engage in sexual activity outside of marriage, as is so common in our society today; whether to accept Christ as Saviour and Lord; whether to tithe and be liberal with offerings to help others and to advance the cause of God; and whether to always think of the spiritual and eternal consequences of each decision.

The Bible speaks of another journey that we all take, even though many hardly give it much thought. It is the spiritual journey toward or away from the heavenly home. Many decide to take that spiritual journey, a journey that begins with an encounter with Jesus Christ. A lasting friendship develops, and the relationship grows closer with each passing year. Each party to the relationship yearns for a face-to-face meeting. Jesus has planned for such an encounter at His second coming.

There is yet a third journey. It is a journey made by the human race through time till it becomes eternity. It is the belief of the author of this book that this journey through time is almost over. We are nearing the second coming of Christ. A look at the abundant evidence available regarding the nearness of that event will dramatically affect the way we view the first two journeys. The way we live our lives today and the direction of our spiritual journey will surely be impacted by an understanding that we are almost home.

Do all roads lead to heaven? Are all denominations guiding folks on the path to the Promised Land? Do the different world religions simply see the eternal realities from different perspectives and are all heading toward the kingdom of God? Is sincerity all that matters? These are not simple questions—but they must be answered by those who are serious about being on the right spiritual road.

Many of us travel for business and pleasure. Frequently we find ourselves in unfamiliar places. When we are far from home we may need assistance to get to our destinations. We must rely on maps or even on counsel from perfect strangers.

For several years my work has required that I travel extensively to speaking appointments and seminars across the United States and Canada. To minimize my stress and to be assured that I can easily find the place of my appointment, I always request written directions from my host. When I pick up my rental car at the airport I always ask for a map. (This map is also helpful in finding where to return the car when the appointment is over!) Then, as a third line of assistance, I always take along my personal Rand McNally road atlas. By using all three aids, I am usually able to find my way. (There are also satellite guidance systems, but I can't afford them!)

There are times, however, when my destination is literally "not on the map." For example, youth camps often are out in the "boonies" by design. Under these circumstances I use the regular maps to get to the city or town that is nearest to the camp and then resort to the written directions sent by my host to make the last few miles.

When you are in unfamiliar territory you can't just use your imagination or your gut instinct as to which way you should go—even if you are blessed with a good sense of direction. The Bible warns, "There is a way that seems right to a man, but its end is the way of death" (Prov. 14:12). If the way that seems right isn't, what does one do? Again the Bible has the answer: "Trust in the Lord with all your heart, and lean not on your own understanding; in all your ways acknowledge Him, and He shall direct your paths" (Prov. 3:5, 6).

One of the truly awesome things about the Incarnation, the birth and life of Christ on earth, is that He came to this earth to show us the way. He said, "I am the way, the truth, and the life. No one comes to the Father except through Me" (John 14:6). The Sermon on the Mount makes plain that each of us has a decision to make—a gate to pass through— and a destination at the end of the road. "Enter by the narrow gate; for wide is the gate and broad is the way that leads to destruction, and there are many who go in by it. Because narrow is the gate and difficult is the way which leads to life, and there are few who find it" (Matt. 7:13, 14).

When Adam and Eve sinned, God responded with love. He let them know of His love by providing clothes for them and outlining the plan of salvation. There was a way out of the mess, but it would take a long time. And yes, there was an immediate price to pay. They had to leave their garden home. They could no longer eat of the tree of life and thereby perpetuate their life of evil. As it was, in the course of his 930 years Adam lived to see the almost total degradation of the race. Late in his life he was, for a time, contemporary with Enoch and Methuselah. Possibly he learned from them of God's plan to destroy the earth with a flood.

To Noah God revealed His plan to save the righteous in an ark. For 120 years Noah's life was one of excitement—anticipating the Flood and building the ark. But it also must have been a life of frustration, for surely his neighbors would have rained on him a constant barrage of criticism, scorn, and ridicule. Yet he saved himself and his family. After the Flood wickedness increased, and God again acted in righteousness, scattering the rebels at the Tower of Babel. But He gathered the righteous into one family through the promise to Abraham.

The call of Abraham, the birth of Isaac, and the experiences of Jacob began the long history of "the people of God." All three of these men made serious mistakes in their lives, yet God has identified Himself since then as the God of Abraham, Isaac, and Jacob.

Later God called Moses to deliver Israel from bondage in Egypt. Moses, who had been adopted into the family of the pharaoh, had to decide between the wealth and pleasures of Egypt or joining with the people of God. He chose the latter, and with God's power delivered Israel and led them to the borders of Canaan.

Inspired by God, Moses wrote the first five books of the Bible. He outlined salvation history from the Creation to the Exodus. He chronicled the giving of God's laws in written form. His writing combines poetry, salvation history, legislation, and exhortation. The three major divisions of the law, as outlined in Deuteronomy 4:44, 45, are the testimonies, the statutes, and the judgments. The moral law is summarized in the Ten Commandments.

The reign of King David, about a thousand years before Christ, was a high point in the experience of ancient Israel, a golden age, the "Camelot" kingdom of a man after God's own heart. But David compromised God's will for Israel, sowing in his own family the seeds of discord that would later divide the kingdom. Later kings led the people into apostasy. Because of increasing worldliness and disobedience, God allowed them to be carried away in captivity to Babylon. There He used faithful young men to represent Him. Daniel, a statesman-prophet, was used by God to outline the course of history from his day to the end of time. The time prophecies of Daniel and those of the apostle John in his Revelation of Jesus Christ give us a picture of where we are in this world's history and what can be expected in the time remaining.

Questioned privately by His disciples, Jesus revealed much about end-time events. He gave a number of "signs of the end," and described events in the world and the church that would indicate His coming was near—at the very doors. In the providence of God this is where we find ourselves today.

There are two indicators that must be considered in determining where we are in the journey to eternity. One is the prophetic time line that is laid out in Scripture. The other indicator is the list of "signs of the end" that has been given by Jesus and the Bible writers. We will consider them in that order in the chapters that follow.

Things are happening in detail just as we have been told that they would. Truly we live in a grand and awful time. It is a time for confidence and trust in the mighty God and His many wonderful promises. My hope is that this book will serve as a call to all Christians to awake and be vigilant.

God has laid out in His Word the links in the prophetic chain that stretch from eternity in the past to eternity in the future. Understanding these prophetic links will help us know where we are today in the procession of the ages and what we may expect in the days ahead. Since all the prophecies that were to be fulfilled by our day are now traced on the pages of history, we may be assured that those Bible predictions that are yet future will be fulfilled in their order. Today the signs of the times tell us that we are standing on the very threshold of eternity.

God commanded Noah, "Come into the ark, you and all your household, because I have seen that you are righteous before Me" (Gen. 7:1). Noah obeyed and was saved. God instructed Lot, "Get up, get out of this place; for the Lord will destroy this city" (Gen. 19:14). Lot placed himself under the guardianship of the heavenly messengers and was saved. In a similar manner Christ's disciples were given warning of the destruction of Jerusalem. Those who watched for the sign of the coming ruin and fled from the city escaped the destruction. And so today we are given the warning of the Second Coming and the end of this world as we know it. Those who heed the warning will be saved.

CHAPTER TWO

CHOOSING THE RIGHT MAP

A bronze plaque set in stone on the top of Springer Mountain in north Georgia reads: "The Appalachian Trail—Georgia to Maine—a footpath for those who seek fellowship with the Wilderness." And so begins (or ends!) America's most popular long-distance trail, the "AT." It stretches 2,150 miles, winding along or close to the summits of the Appalachian Mountains. It involves 14 Eastern states, from Springer Mountain in Georgia to Mount Katahdin in Maine.

The AT was the vision of Benton MacKaye and others who kicked the idea around for more than 10 years. In 1921 MacKaye took the initiative and launched the project through an article in *The Journal of the American Institute of Architects.* The work of marking the trail and clearing the way was completed in 1937 when the Civilian Conservation Corp (CCC) workers cut the last two miles of trail on a high ridge connecting Spaulding and Sugarloaf mountains in Maine.

In April 1948 Earl Shaffer packed his Mountain Troop rucksack and headed for Georgia. "The Long Cruise," as Shaffer referred to his trip, started on Mount Oglethorpe and ended some four months and 2,050 miles later on top of Mount Katahdin; it earned him the distinction of being the AT's first "thru-hiker." He through-hiked the entire Appalachian Trail again in 1998, just a few weeks before his eightieth birthday, thereby setting another distinctive record—the oldest person ever to do so.

In 1948 many considered Shaffer's through-hike a stunt, but the dream of long-distance hiking has become a fever since then and has spawned other long-distance trails, including the Pacific Crest Trail, which runs from Mexico to Canada.

The Appalachian Trail Conference, with headquarters in Harpers Ferry, West Virginia, reports that each year a little more than 3,000 people set out to "thru-hike" the trail. Only about 10 percent of them make it the whole way in a single year; the other 90 percent must leave their dreams by the wayside. This happens for a number of reasons, but mostly because the trail turns out to be more than they bargained for.

In their interesting and helpful book, *The Appalachian Trail Backpacker,* Victoria and Frank Logue suggest that before attempting to through-hike the trail you should ask yourself the following questions:

- Will completing the trail be worth being wet/cold/hot day after day?
- Can I wear the same dirty clothes for days on end?
- Can I go without a bath, sometimes for as long as a week?
- Can I withstand the physical pain that often accompanies backpacking?
- Can I stand being away from my home/relationships for four to six months?
- Is the idea of through-hiking the AT my all-consuming desire? Am I willing for it to be?
- Am I afraid of the outdoors—insects, animals, sleeping outdoors night after night?

These points remind me of the text in Matthew 24:13: "But he who endures to the end shall be saved." Endurance and a good map are two primary ingredients to success.

My son, Andrew, and I have become "section hikers" on the Appalachian Trail. Instead of doing a "thru-hike" in one year, we are doing sections of the trail as time permits, with the goal of completing it over a period of several years. For example, during the Christmas break of 1998 we hiked together through the entire state of Maryland—from Pen-Mar, Pennsylvania, on the Mason-Dixon line to Harpers Ferry, West Virginia. It is approximately 40 miles of ridge hiking, but we had to cover more than 14 miles per day, including side trips to our overnight sleeping spots. The first night we pitched our tent at Pogo Springs primitive campsite.

We had made arrangements to spend the second

night in a primitive log cabin owned by the Potomac Appalachian Trail Club. Its only advantage over our tent was that it had a woodstove inside. As our second day on the trail neared its end and the sun was setting, we reached the summit of Lamb's Knoll mountain and passed the FAA communication tower. We still had about two miles to go. We hiked on for another 30 minutes in the twilight.

The Appalachian Trail is marked with white blazes on trees and rocks. The blazes are two inches wide and six inches high and are usually about eye level. We watched for a blue-blazed side trail that would lead off to our left at the point of a rock over-look and take us to the Bear Spring cabin, seven tenths of a mile off the AT. Our trail guidebook stated that this trail was rough and steep. We found the description to be quite accurate. In December the leaves are all down and trails that are not used very often tend to blend with the rest of the forest floor. We put on our headlamps and started following the blue blazes to the cabin. If it hadn't been for the blazes we never would have found it.

The Appalachian Trail Club produces detailed maps and guidebooks for those who wish to use them. With their assistance it is well-nigh impossible to get lost. Wouldn't it be nice if Christians had such help? Fortunately, we do! We have the Bible and the continuing guidance of the Holy Spirit, whose job it is to guide us into all truth.

A Guidebook for the Narrow Way

Life is a journey, and the Christian life is described just that way in John Bunyan's *Pilgrim's Progress.* To follow the King's highway to heaven is a metaphor indicating that the problems of life are really only encounters along the way. To understand the journey and find the way accurately, we need a map. The Bible is that map. An unknown author described the Guidebook this way: "This book contains the mind of God, the state of man, the way of salvation, the doom of sinners, and the happiness of believers. Its doctrines are holy, its precepts are binding, its histories are true, and its decisions are immutable. Read it to be wise, believe it to be safe, and practice it to be holy. It contains light to direct you, food to support you, and comfort to cheer you. It is the traveler's map, the pilgrim's staff, the pilot's compass, the soldier's sword, and the Christian's charter. Here paradise is restored, heaven opened, and the gates of hell disclosed. Christ is its grand object, our good its design, and the glory of God its end. It should fill the memory, rule the heart, and guide the feet. Read it slowly, frequently, and prayerfully. It is a mine of wealth, a paradise of glory, and a river of pleasure. It is given to you in life, will be opened in the judgment, and will be remembered forever. It involves the highest responsibility, will reward the greatest labor, and will condemn all who trifle with its sacred contents."

These are grand statements about the Bible, the Book of books. The Bible continues to be published around the world by the millions of copies, yet how few people are led to a study of its message and transformed by the power of God to obey its precepts. In preparation for this book I collected more than 1,000 pages of information on the Bible: there are the statements of others, Bible texts, Bible studies, etc. An entire book could be written on the subject of Bible study, and thousands have been. But in the interest of brevity I have decided just to share my personal testimony in the pages that follow, and encourage you to find your own 1,000 pages of information. It will bless your soul. In Bible study the joy is in the journey *and* the destination!

Why I Believe the Bible Is God's Word

There are many questions in life: How do we know for sure what life is all about? How can we know what truth is? How do we really know which philosophy of life to believe and practice? I believe the Bible has an answer to all these questions. But how can we know that the Bible is true—that it is really the Word of God? After all, life is too short and serious to take the wrong road.

In my study I have found seven reasons that I believe the Bible is the Word of God. When you read it as God's authoritative Word you have a true standard upon which to function, to believe, to plan, to hope. You won't just take the word of others. You won't just believe the Bible out of a lack of options—an easy way out. You can use your reason—your God-given reason—to prove its claims. But taken together, the cumulative evidence is unmatched by any other philosophy, book, or way of life. All other options leave so much unanswered.

1. The Bible answers life's basic questions. This is

not just philosophy; it is the basic fact of existence. It is reasonable to ask things such as: Is there a God? What is truth? Where did I come from? Why am I here? And where am I going? What is it like after here?

If there is a God, He will reveal Himself. I believe that the cumulative evidence of these points proves that there is a God and that He has revealed Himself in many ways. We can understand that God exists through the study of nature and science, His providential leadings, the inspiration of His Word, answered prayers, fulfilled promises, fulfilled prophecies, etc.

In addition, there should be some normative answers to basic questions. I ask, *Where did I come from?* I get the answer, "In the beginning God created . . ." God is my Creator. *Why am I here?* Because God created me, loved me, and has a plan for my life. He wants me to live with Him—now and forever. *And where am I going?* I am going home! He has prepared a place for those who believe in Him and trust Him. That place will be in heaven for a while, and then He will create a new earth to be our final home. Many ask and wonder if there is consciousness beyond this life. Life is a journey, and when it is over, people rest in their graves in a state of unconsciousness until there is a great resurrection, when all who have followed God's way of salvation will be restored to life. They will then join with the faithful who are alive at the end of earth's history. The two groups will go together to be with the Lord. There they are freed from sorrow, pain, and death. These are the answers my Bible gives to life's basic questions.

2. The Bible presents history in an honest manner. We all have our biases. We see our own lives in the best possible light. In general, a person writing an autobiography tends to remember and record mostly positive things. When a friend writes a biography the result again is quite positive. On the other hand, if a politician were to write a biography of an opponent, for example, we could expect a result that would be quite different.

The Bible seems to present humanity in an open and honest manner. Even the stars of the Bible—its main characters—are portrayed warts and all. The stories of Adam, Noah, Moses, Abraham, David, the disciples of Jesus, and Paul tell of their frailties as well as their strong points. In fact, sometimes their faults may be more fully presented than their virtues. This has been a subject of wonder to many, and has given infidels occasion to scoff at the Bible. But one of the strongest evidences of the truth of Scripture is that the facts are not glossed over, that the sins of its chief characters are not suppressed. We are more likely to be getting the truth this way.

3. The Bible has an inner consistency. The Bible was written over a 1,600-year period, extending from the time of Moses, about 1,500 years before Christ, to the disciple John, who wrote about A.D. 100. Its authors differed widely in rank and occupation, in mental and spiritual endowments, and levels of education. Yet, taken as a whole, it presents a remarkable harmony. The truths that it presents meet the wants and needs of people in all circumstances and experiences of life.

4. The Bible has been preserved over a 3,500-year period essentially unchanged. When one considers all that could have happened to the Bible during its history it is obvious that only by divine intervention has it been kept intact. Consider, for example, that for nearly 3,000 years—from 1500 B.C. to A.D. 1450, when printing was invented—the Bible was preserved and reproduced by hand! In addition, some of those who preserved and copied it during the Middle Ages did not even understand what they were copying! Yet it was preserved essentially error-free.

5. The Bible's accuracy is confirmed by archaeology. The past 150 years have witnessed the birth, growth, and phenomenal development of the science of biblical archaeology. This science has performed many wonders in furnishing background material and illustrating, illuminating, and in many cases authenticating the message and meaning of the Old and New Testament Scriptures. Think of just a few of these evidences.

The Rosetta stone, now in the British Museum in London, was discovered in 1799 at Rosetta (Rashid), near the westernmost mouth of the Nile River, by an officer in Napoleon's expedition to Egypt. It is a slab of black basalt with an inscription written on it in three languages—all telling the same story. The discovery of this stone was the key that unlocked the door to knowledge of the language and literature of ancient Egypt. The three languages on the stone were Greek and two forms of Egyptian writing—the older, more complicated hieroglyphic script and the later simplified and more popular demotic writing, the common language of the people. Many artifacts from ancient Egypt had been found before that contained the hieroglyphic writing, but no one had ever been able to make any sense of it. Inasmuch as the Greek writing on the stone could be read by many scholars, it became the code-breaker for the Egyptian languages!

The Moabite stone was another amazing discovery. This important artifact, found in 1868, dates from about 850 B.C. It is a stele or monument—an inscribed stone. It was erected by Mesha, king of Moab, and is also called the Mesha stone. It tells about the wars of Mesha of Moab with Omri, king of Israel, and Omri's successors. The material recorded on this stone parallels biblical history recorded in 2 Kings 1 and 3. Many places mentioned in the Old Testament are noted on the Moabite stone.

The Dead Sea scrolls were the greatest archaeological discovery of modern times. In 1947 a young Bedouin shepherd came upon a cave near Qumran, south of Jericho, that contained many leather scrolls and some 600 fragmentary inscriptions in Hebrew and Aramaic writing. The scrolls had been sealed in clay vessels. After intensive study of those manuscripts and others found subsequently in the area, scholars were able to date them to a period ranging from about 300 B.C. to 30 B.C.

The material contained both Old Testament and intertestamental documents. Included are two rolls of Isaiah (one complete), most of the first two chapters of Habakkuk, and fragments of *all* the Old Testament books except Esther. The Isaiah scroll, among the initial finds, has remained the best known of the discoveries. It is about 1,000 years older than the most ancient Hebrew text, the Masoretic, previously known. In fact, the Dead Sea scrolls are the oldest existing manuscripts of the Bible in any language. Amazingly, the text of Isaiah is essentially the same as we have today! To my mind this is a matter of divine providence.

6. *The Bible's prophecies come true!* All of us are curious about the future. But who really knows what will happen tomorrow? Of course, only God does. The Bible makes many predictions both as to time and to events. If the Bible is true, these predictions should come true. And they do! How can the Bible be a collection of myths, as some say? Let me share with you what the Bible says of itself. Then we can mention a few of its prophecies and their fulfillment. Peter said, "For we did not follow cunningly devised fables when we made known to you the power and coming of our Lord Jesus Christ, but were eyewitnesses of His majesty. For He received from God the Father honor and glory when such a voice came to Him from the Excellent Glory: 'This is My beloved Son, in whom I am well pleased.' And we heard this voice which came from heaven when we were with Him on the holy mountain. And so we have the prophetic word confirmed, which you do well to heed as a light that shines in a dark place, until the day dawns and the morning star rises in your hearts; knowing this first, that no prophecy of Scripture is of any private interpretation, for prophecy never came by the will of man, but holy men of God spoke as they were moved by the Holy Spirit" (2 Peter 1:16-21).

With this background I'll just list a few time prophecies and their fulfillment. God told Noah that humankind would have only 120 more years and that Noah should build an ark. The Flood came and took all but Noah and his family. God told Abraham that his descendants would be afflicted in a strange land 400 years, but that then they would come out with great substance. First they were afflicted in Canaan, then in Egypt. When they left Egypt centuries later they did indeed bring treasure with them.

God predicted through His prophet Jeremiah that because of Israel's disobedience they would be taken captive by the Babylonians and would be held for 70 years. It happened! God told Daniel, while he was a captive in Babylon, when the Messiah would be born. When the time came He was born—in Bethlehem, as another prophet predicted! The list could go on. The most interesting point about prophecy is that since we have seen the other prophecies fulfilled we can know that those yet to be fulfilled will come true as well. That's why we know we are almost home!

7. *The Bible's divine origin is proved by the testimony of transformed lives.* I guess you could say that the proof is in the pudding. The Bible claims to have the ability by the power of God to reclaim human beings from sin and degradation and give them a positive and more abundant life. Is it true? I have seen it happen many times. It is the testimony of my own life! Where would I be today without the guidance of God's Word?

What kind of people get involved in sharing their time and resources in helping others? Is it the worldly and self-abusers? No, it is those who follow the example of Jesus. If everyone practiced the principles taught in the Bible, we would not have to lock anything. The streets in every city would be safe. There would be no need for a prison system. Those who follow God's Word are a living testimony of its divine origin.

The Great Standard of Truth

The seven points I have listed above could all be greatly expanded. However, they are the simple basis for my belief in the authenticity of the Bible as the revealed will of the Creator God. To me the Scriptures are the standard for my faith and practice as a Christian. There can be no other. The more we get to know about God through the study of His Word the deeper our understanding of His will and purpose for our lives. "The fear of the Lord is the beginning of wisdom, and the knowledge of the Holy One is understanding" (Prov. 9:10).

To the Christian the Bible is not just one influence among many others—it is supreme, the ultimate standard of truth.

The Bible says of itself, that it is true. "Sanctify them by Your truth, Your word is truth" (John 17:17). God's law is the truth (Ps. 119:142). Jesus said, "I am the way, the truth, and the life" (John 14:6). Since God and His Word are truth, that must be our ultimate and only standard. Even the Holy Spirit, called the Spirit of Truth, has the purpose of guiding us into all truth—to help us better understand the truth of God's Word. We are told in 1 John 4:1 to try or test the spirits. And what is the standard for testing them? The Bible, of course! It is always the only standard for the Christian. To submit all to the authority of Scripture is what Christianity does as part of its calling. Its teachings are truth, not options. They are the standard and must be obeyed.

Problems Without a Standard

Many Christians today have been taught that the Bible is not the ultimate standard—that church traditions have equal weight with it. But Jesus said that we worship Him in vain when we teach for doctrines the commandments of humans (see Matt. 15:9 and Mark 7:7). He also stated we can make void His law by our traditions (see Matt. 15:3, 6 and Mark 7:8, 13). Unfortunately, many of those who claim to take the Bible as their standard hold their own opinions and preconceptions above the plain teaching of Scripture.

Another common perspective on the value of the Word of God was expressed this way by pop-music icon and actress Madonna: "I want my daughter to read the Bible, but I will explain to her that these are stories that people made up to teach people—it's not the rule" (quoted in *World,* Jan. 18, 1997).

What would happen if people actually immersed themselves in the Bible and studied its message for themselves? Let me give you the testimony of one man who did just that. At the age of 34 William Miller, a farmer and businessman, considered himself a deist. That is, he believed in natural law and morality but denied the existence of a Creator. He decided to study the Bible just to see what it had to say. Here is his report in one paragraph:

"I saw that the Bible did bring to view just such a Saviour as I needed; and I was perplexed to find how an uninspired book should develop principles so perfectly adapted to the wants of a fallen world. I was constrained to admit that the Scriptures must be a revelation from God. *They became my delight; and in Jesus I found a friend.* The Saviour became to me the chiefest among ten thousand; and the Scriptures, which before were dark and contradictory, now became the lamp to my feet and light to my path. My mind became settled and satisfied. I found the Lord God to be a Rock in the midst of the ocean of life. The Bible now became my chief study, and I can truly say, I searched it with great delight. I found the half was never told me. I wondered why I had not seen its beauty and glory before, and marveled that I could have ever rejected it. I found everything revealed that my heart could desire, and a remedy for every disease of the soul. I lost all taste for other reading, and applied my heart to get wisdom from God" (*The Great Controversy,* p. 319; italics supplied). What a testimony! Maybe you too have found the Bible to be such a rich source of hope and confidence!

Jesus and the New Testament writers accepted the Hebrew Scriptures as having unquestioned authority. We are familiar with Paul's reminder to the young man, Timothy: "From childhood you have known the Holy Scriptures, which are able to make you wise for salvation through faith which is in Christ Jesus. All Scripture is given by inspiration of God, and is profitable for doctrine, for reproof, for correction, for instruction in righteousness, that the man of God may be complete, thoroughly equipped for every good work" (2 Tim. 3:15-17). And Peter assures us that prophecy does not come from human sources, but "holy men of God spoke as they were moved by the Holy Spirit" (2 Peter 1:21).

Christians have a tremendous responsibility not only to be deep students of the Word ourselves but also to foster a back-to-the-Bible movement that will help ourselves and our fellow believers prepare for the great tests that we will face in the last great crisis.

Because the Bible is the Word of God, when we study it we actually have an encounter with God. He is speaking to us in His Word! A daily study of the Scriptures has an uplifting influence on the spirit and a broadening influence on the mind.

Dead Wrong

On May 7, 1999, during the bombing of Belgrade, Yugoslavia, by NATO forces in an effort to get Serb forces out of Kosovo, the pilots of a B-2 bomber took aim at the Serbs' Federal Directorate of Supply and Procurement building. Seconds later they dropped three 2,000-pound bombs and scored a direct hit. Mission accomplished. But wait—they were using an outdated map. Someone had failed to note that a year earlier the Chinese Embassy had moved into the building. All the current tourist maps in town had the Chinese Embassy at its new location, but the CIA and the Pentagon had used an old map by mistake. The result: several Chinese journalists were killed and 20 embassy workers were wounded. And of course, there was significant collateral damage.

Thousands of Chinese demonstrated for days in front of the U.S. Embassy in Beijing. They broke out most of the windows in the ambassador's residence and the embassy by throwing rocks, Molotov cocktails, and paint. This situation put ambassador James Sasser, his wife, and his staff in real fear for their lives. All because of the use of the wrong map!

Using the wrong map can and does have fatal consequences. But when such consequences involve our eternal life, the stakes are at their highest. The Bible is the only reliable map when we are seeking our eternal destiny. Let's make sure we keep ours close by and follow it only.

CHAPTER THREE

TRUTH MATTERS

There are many voices calling people today. There is New Age, astrology, science fiction, Eastern religions, materialism, Communism, and much more. But God has given ample evidence to the reasonable person that His Word is true and can be trusted as the standard for faith and practice. He desires that those who worship Him do so in spirit and in truth. Truth is the first item listed in the armor of God (Eph. 6:14). Accordingly, the Bible and the Bible only must be our standard for all doctrines and the basis of all reforms.

The opinions of wise and educated people; the deductions of science; the creeds or decisions of ecclesiastical councils, no matter what church they represent; the voice of the majority—none of these alone or in any combination should be regarded as evidence for or against any point of religious faith. Before we accept any doctrine or teaching we should demand a plain explanation from the Bible for its support!

We must be a part of that people who stand on the foundation of truth—"Thy word is truth." It is not bigotry or self-righteousness to share with others what one believes to be the truth. In fact, it is quite selfish not to do so. If a person doesn't believe that their church tradition is teaching the truth, they should prayerfully search for one that does. We are encouraged to speak "the truth in love" (Eph. 4:15), but it must be spoken. Paul asks, "Have I therefore become your enemy because I tell you the truth?" (Gal. 4:16).

No doubt our daily prayer should be that of King David: "Teach me Your way, O Lord; I will walk in Your truth; unite my heart to fear Your name" (Ps. 86:11).

We can recognize the significance of life's journey and where we are in the stream of time only as we seriously consider the Word of God, which He says is truth (see John 17:17). In their haste to bring about worldwide Christian unity there are those who belittle others who are reluctant to drop their long-held beliefs. We all possess a limited knowledge of the world around us. We can become "experts" in only a few things at a time. So of course it is not possible for anyone to say they know the "truth," the complete facts, about anything. But when it comes to spiritual things and the way to our eternal destiny, God has given us the directions in His Word and through His life, both of which He says are truth. In spiritual things, then, by the grace of God we can know what is truth. Truth is what God says it is. We have His word on that.

Unity at What Price?

Unity was a high priority with Jesus. It was painful to Him that even after He had told His disciples that He would soon die, they were still arguing over who would be the greatest among them. After participating with them in the Last Supper, Jesus had a long and serious talk with them about the immediate and distant future. It is in this setting that John records for us the longest recorded prayer of Jesus. He prayed for Himself, His disciples, and then for all the believers.

In His prayer Jesus looked down through the ages to the church and the end of time, and He prayed for unity! He also prayed for unity among His disciples. It was after they had come into full unity that the Holy Spirit was poured out upon them in full measure.

Jesus promised that when He went back to heaven He would send the Spirit with His general and special gifts. In Ephesians 4 we learn that the gifts were to bring about unity of faith and to solidify doctrines so that believers are not tossed on the waves of uncertainty.

Unity does not come naturally to the unconverted heart. It takes the indwelling of God's Spirit to bring this about.

Truth is basic to real unity. In Jesus' "unity" prayer of John 17 He prayed, "Sanctify them by Your truth. Your word is truth" (verse 17). This most touching and wonderful prayer reaches down through the ages, even to our day, for His words were: "I do not pray for these alone, but also for those who will believe in Me through their word" (verse 20).

Unity in Diversity

We are all as different as snowflakes. We have different backgrounds, different personality types, different ways of looking at things, yet in Christ we can be one in purpose. We can learn to love one another. The disciples were a very diverse group, yet in Christ and by His Spirit they formed a team that changed the world. It is important to note that not until they submitted to the infilling of the Spirit of Christ did they really become effective in their witnessing.

One distinguishing characteristic of God's true people at the end of time will be the racial harmony that will exist among them. We must all pray earnestly that our inherited and cultivated prejudices will be taken away so that the world will recognize our love for one another and give God the glory.

We know that there is a great work before us. As Jesus told the repentant Peter, when we are converted we are to strengthen others. With God's promised blessing mighty things will happen. The closer we come to Christ the closer we will come to each other and the more focused will be our religious experience. We must understand that the secret of true unity in the church and in the family is not diplomacy, not management, not a superhuman effort to overcome difficulties—though there will be much of this to do—but union with Christ.

The Bonds of Christian Fellowship

As we get closer to the end of our spiritual journey our Christian friends will be the closest people to us on earth. The bond between Christians will be cemented by the Spirit of God. Some have been abandoned by family members as a result of their Christian commitment. As Jesus said, they become our brothers and sisters. These people will love to gather together for Christian fellowship, and in fact are encouraged to do so. "Not forsaking the assembling of ourselves together, as is the manner of some, but exhorting one another, and so much the more as you see the Day approaching" (Heb. 10:25).

Each of us should show our interest in the prosperity of the church by identifying ourselves with it and working with our fellow believers in the completion of the work of the Great Commission to carry the gospel to all the world. Precisely because unity is such a positive blessing to the church and a witness to the world, Satan works to bring about division.

Unity in the Larger Picture

Yes, unity is important. The unity that Christ spoke of was unity of faith and doctrine based on the platform of truth. True unity can never be at the expense of truth. Truth is more important than unity. It is the work of God's Spirit to bring unity. The Spirit also guides us into all truth. Accordingly, we can't have Spirit-inspired unity apart from truth.

There are many calls for Christians today to join some great ecumenical church or to drop "denominational barriers" and become one happy Christian family. On the surface this sounds great, but let us remember that God has called the church in the last days to uphold unity on the platform of truth. The last message to the world and those in apostate religions is to "come out of her, My people" (Rev. 18:4). Jesus prayed that His followers might be one; but we are not to sacrifice the truth in order to secure this union, for we are to be sanctified through the truth.

Truth is the foundation of all real peace. Human wisdom would pronounce this basis too narrow. Humans would try to effect unity through concession to popular opinion through compromise with the world, a sacrifice of vital godliness. But truth is God's basis for the unity of His people.

In February 1996 nearly 40,000 ministers of many denominations met as part of the Promise Keepers organization in the Georgia Dome in Atlanta. The theme for all the Promise Keeper rallies in 1996 was "Breaking Down the Walls," referring to the walls of racism and denominationalism. Promise Keepers' founder, Bill McCartney, called for cooperation among religious groups. "Contention between denominations has gone on long enough," he said. "If the church ever stood together, . . . God would have his way" (*Christianity Today,* Apr. 8, 1996). Many other presenters, such as Max Lucado, presented similar sentiments.

Centuries ago, when faithful Christians were faced with compromise in the church, they had a painful decision to make. It cost some their lives, but they felt they had no alternative. After a long and severe conflict, a few decided to dissolve all union with the apostate church if it still refused to free itself from falsehood and idolatry. They saw that separation was an absolute necessity if they were to obey the Word of God. They dared not tolerate errors fatal to their own souls and set an example that would imperil the faith of their children and children's children. To secure peace and unity they were ready to make any concession consistent with fidelity to God; but they felt that even peace would be too dearly purchased at the sacrifice of principle. They concluded that if unity could be secured only by the compromise of truth and righteousness, then let there be difference and even war.

This is not an easy issue to deal with, and must be handled with great care. Bible-believing Christians do not want to appear aloof—however, we must insist that truth be the basis of unity.

Let us pray for wisdom, kindness, and firmness as we deal with the implementation of Christ's prayer for unity. "Sanctify them by Your truth. Your word is truth" (John 17:17).

Truth and Tradition

There are good traditions and there are bad traditions, just as there are good and bad habits. We can know the difference by the standard of Bible truth. It is by the Bible that we know which teachings are right. Both Old and New Testaments tell us this. "To the law and to the testimony! If they do not speak according to this word, it is because there is no light in them" (Isa. 8:20). "All Scripture is given by inspiration of God, and is profitable for doctrine, for reproof, for correction, for instruction in righteousness" (2 Tim. 3:16).

We are all eager to be guided by God's Spirit. But there are also evil spirits, and so we are counseled, "Do not believe every spirit, but test the spirits, whether they are of God; because many false prophets have gone out into the world" (1 John 4:1). So we should test teachings and spirits by God's Word. But what about tradition? Yes, Scripture pulls rank on everything! That is always our standard of last resort. Those who put tradition above Scripture Jesus called hypocrites! "Well did Isaiah prophesy of you hypocrites, as it is written: 'This people honors Me with their lips, but their heart is far from Me. And in vain they worship Me, teaching as doctrines the commandments of men.' For laying aside the commandment of God, you hold the tradition of men" (Mark 7:6-8). We must be certain, as we prepare to meet our Saviour and share our faith with others, that our religious experience is founded not on traditions but on Scripture.

Truth's Practical Application

With the enormous emphasis today on ecumenism and the push to break down denominational walls, much more study should be given to the topic of the church, to what scholars call ecclesiology. On what basis should one become a member of a church? Is it a compromise to be a member of a denomination, or should I just be a part of the "church at large" and fellowship with some nondenominational group?

Apparently church was God's idea. He organized

it. The New Testament is full of the evidence—with apostles, elders, deacons, gifts, fellowship, and more. The Lord blessed the efforts of the early church: "And the Lord added to the church daily those who were being saved" (Acts 2:47). Barnabas, one of the early church leaders, went to Tarsus to find Paul. "And when he had found him, he brought him to Antioch. So it was that for a whole year they assembled with the church and taught a great many people. And the disciples were first called Christians in Antioch" (Acts 11:26). The church was a close-knit and vibrant group.

When Peter was thrown in prison, constant prayer was offered to God for him by the church. The church organized a prayer vigil. There was a group praying 24 hours a day for his deliverance. They were praying for one of their leaders! Further, God gave "gifts" to the church. He wanted the church to benefit. "And God has appointed these in the church: first apostles, second prophets, third teachers, after that miracles, then gifts of healings, helps, administrations, varieties of tongues" (1 Cor. 12:28). The gifts were to be manifested to "edify" the church (see 1 Cor. 14:12).

"Christ loved the church, and gave Himself for her" (Eph. 5:25). There is a close connection between Christ and His church. He is the vine—the church members are the branches. He is the head—the church members with their various gifts are the body. He is the cornerstone—the church members are the living stones. He is the bridegroom—the church is the bride. Accordingly, there is a very close and sacred relationship between Christ and His church. Connection with Christ, then, involves connection with His church. And since the church was organized for service, when we are connected with Christ we will live a life of service.

Many years ago a person with much experience observed that all church members were involved with their respective churches for one of three reasons. Over the years I have noted the truth of his observations. Here are the reasons:

1. Most people are members of a particular church because they were raised in that church. Their family have been members for years. They were born in that church. They were dedicated or baptized in that church. Perhaps they were married in that church. Almost all of their close friends are in that church.

2. Another common reason is convenience. For example, let's say that a Baptist and a Methodist get married. They are not going to be members of both churches or alternate between them on Sundays. Most of the time one will join the other's church out of convenience, and that is the end of the story. Another example of convenience is a person who is a member of the Congregational Church in New England, let us say, and moves to Alabama. Not finding a Congregational church nearby, this person joins the nearest church, which may be Presbyterian.

3. The third reason for church membership is quite different from the first two. This reason involves personal belief. A person decides to study the Bible in an effort to determine what it says and means. This may be a private, personal study, or with

a group, seminar, or evangelistic meeting. Once a basic knowledge of God and His will is discovered, the person seeks fellowship with those who follow what the Scriptures teach. This reason for church membership involves theology—what a person understands about God and His will.

In my personal judgment this is the only justifiable reason for being a church member. Membership that is based on an understanding of truth rather than heritage or convenience is the only biblical reason.

Truth Matters

In the controversy between truth and error the last great conflict will be between the laws of human beings and the law of God. We are now entering onto this battlefield. This battle is not between rival churches contending for the supremacy, but between the religion of the Bible and the religions of fable and tradition. The agencies that have united against truth are now actively at work. God's holy Word, which has been handed down to us at so great a cost of suffering and bloodshed, is little valued. There are very few who really accept it as the rule of life. Infidelity prevails to an alarming extent, not just in the world but in the church as well. Many who call themselves Christians have come to deny doctrines that are the very pillars of the Christian faith. The great facts of Creation as presented by the inspired writers, the fall of humanity, the atonement, the perpetuity of God's law—these are practically rejected by many who are professedly Christian.

But thank God, millions of men, women, and

young people are sincerely asking, "What is truth?" And to those who really want to know, Jesus says, "I am the way, the truth, and the life. No one comes to the Father except through Me" (John 14:6). Again, in His prayer to His Father, Jesus said, "And this is eternal life, that they may know You, the only true God, and Jesus Christ whom You have sent" (John 17:3).

John, in his First Epistle, used very pointed language to emphasize the value of truth. "He who says, 'I know Him,' and does not keep His commandments, is a liar, and the truth is not in him" (1 John 2:4). In the mind of God, obedience to the commandments and the way of truth are one and the same. It should be for us as well.

CHAPTER FOUR

FAITHFUL GUIDES

Her name was Sacagawea. She was the only woman among some 40 men on the most famous expedition in the New World, the Lewis and Clark exploration of western America. The expedition began on May 14, 1804, in St. Louis. The trip to the Pacific Ocean and back covered more than 8,000 miles and ended two and a half years later, on September 23, 1806.

A Shoshoni Indian, Sacagawea joined the expedition as guide and interpreter, taking it through land never before seen by White people. Crossing the Continental Divide, the explorers met relatives of Sacagawea. From them she was able to get food and horses needed to continue the journey. In the Rocky and Bitterroot mountains the explorers encountered such difficult terrain that they frequently walked and used their horses as pack animals.

Sacagawea has been honored by having a river, a peak, and a mountain pass named after her. Monuments and memorials in her honor stand in five Western states. She was a faithful guide and likely the most important person in the expedition party.

I have emphasized our spiritual journey in this book, as it is a biblical illustration and one that is familiar to many people. Since we know where we want to go but don't know the way on our own, it is critical for success that we have a guide—one that we can trust with our lives. Guidance can come from many sources, but which ones can we trust?

Divine Guidance

God has provided us with three sources of guidance. They are His Word, the Bible; the life of Jesus; and the Holy Spirit. We have already established the credibility of the Bible. One of its inspired authors says, "Your word is a lamp to my feet and a light to my path" (Ps. 119:105). Jesus said of Himself, "I am the way, the truth, and the life. No one comes to the Father except through Me" (John 14:6). On another occasion He said, "I am the light of the world. He who follows Me shall not walk in darkness, but have the light of life" (John 8:12).

In Old Testament times God had promised, "I will instruct you and teach you in the way you should go; I will guide you with My eye" (Ps. 32:8). God was in essence telling them, "I will keep My eye on you." Apparently at the time of the exodus from Egypt God had become personally involved in the guidance of His people. The Bible records, "And the Lord went before them by day in a pillar of cloud to lead the way, and by night a pillar of fire to give them light, so as to go by day and night. He did not take away the pillar of cloud by day or the pillar of fire by night from before the people" (Ex. 13:21, 22).

The Bible always urges us to find truth, which, as we have noted, is found in God and His Word. But Jesus told His disciples that He would send the Holy Spirit as a guide or interpreter of the Scriptures. "When, He, the Spirit of truth, has come, He will guide you into all truth; for He will not speak on His own authority, but whatever He hears He will speak; and He will tell you things to come. He will glorify Me, for He will take of what is Mine [God's Word] and declare it to you" (John 16:13, 14).

Accordingly, any "spirit" that leads away from God's Word or speaks things that are not in harmony with the Bible is not the Holy Spirit that was promised to those who seek truth. Thus the Bible warns, "Beloved, do not believe every spirit, but test the spirits, whether they are of God; because many false prophets have gone out into the world" (1 John 4:1). Our task is not simply to be looking for the narrow road to heaven; we must also be on guard against Satan's counterfeits of our divine guides. The Bible describes him as "a roaring lion, seeking whom he may devour" (1 Peter 5:8). The devil's major tool is deception. From the time he deceived Eve in the Garden of Eden he has used this as his most effective tool.

Jesus warned us again and again to beware of deception. In Matthew 24 He waves the red flag of warning no less than four times.

1. "Take heed that no one deceives you" (verse 4).

2. "For many will come in My name, saying, 'I am Christ,' and will deceive many" (verse 5).

3. "Then many false prophets will rise up and deceive many" (verse 11).

4. "For false christs and false prophets will rise and show great signs and wonders to deceive, if possible, even the elect" (verse 24).

Let's consider ourselves warned!

Blind and False Guides

Though they may not know it, some who look, talk, and act like sincere ministers are really doing the devil's work. They may be ever so nice and helpful, but if they are sharing tradition only and are not speaking the truth based on God's Word, they are false prophets. "Beware of false prophets, who come to you in sheep's clothing, but inwardly they are ravenous wolves" (Matt. 7:15). Jesus called the Pharisees, who were a part of the religious leadership of His day, "blind guides" (see Matt. 23:16, 24). It was in this context that He accused them of straining out gnats but swallowing a camel. In other words, they majored in minors and ignored or overlooked, sometimes for money, more serious offenses.

Today, as then, there are false spiritual guides to whose doctrines many listen eagerly. It is Satan's studied effort to divert minds from the hope of salvation through faith in Christ and obedience to the law of God. In every age the archenemy adapts his temptations to the prejudices or inclinations of those whom he is seeking to deceive. In the days of Jesus and the apostles he led the Jews to exalt the ceremonial law and reject Christ; today he induces many professing Christians, under pretense of honoring Christ, to cast contempt on the moral law and to teach that its precepts may be transgressed with impunity. It is a moral duty of everyone who claims to be a child of God to withstand firmly any perverters of the faith and by God's Word to fearlessly expose their errors.

Satan is so subtle that he tries to focus our attention on humanity in the place of God and His Word. He leads people to look to priests, bishops, pastors, rabbis, and professors of theology as their guides, instead of searching the Scriptures to learn the truth for themselves. By controlling the minds of some leaders he can influence many followers according to his will.

The Work of Angels

Many times in the history of God's dealings with humankind He has used angels as "ministering spirits" to guide His people. In that well-known chapter of promised protection, Psalm 91, we are told, "He shall give His angels charge over you, to keep you in all your ways" (verse 11). Not until we are able to see in the light of eternity will we understand the extent of care that God has given us through the work of angels. From studying the Bible we know that these heavenly beings take an active part in the affairs of human beings. They have appeared in garments that shone as the lightning; they have come in the appearance of humans, in the dress of travelers. They have accepted the hospitality of human homes; they have acted as guides to weary travelers. They have protected God's people and turned aside the weapons of the destroyer.

Feelings, Impressions, and Opinions as Guides

The Bible has answers to sincere questions about whether we can depend on our feelings, impressions, and opinions for guidance on our spiritual journey. Though God may guide us in His providence after we have studied His Word, when we are seeking answers it is best to go directly to His book. Solomon, whom God blessed with wisdom and inspiration, said, "Trust in the Lord with all your heart, and lean not on your own understanding; in all your ways acknowledge Him, and He shall direct your paths. Do not be wise in your own eyes; fear the Lord and depart from evil. It will be health to your flesh, and strength to your bones" (Prov. 3:5-8).

Impressions and feelings are no sure evidence that a person is being led by the Lord. Satan will, if he is unsuspected, give feelings and impressions. Therefore these are not correct and safe guides. We must become thoroughly familiar with God's Word so that we are able to have a "Thus said the Lord" answer for our questions and to examine our feelings.

God Is Leading "a People"

While it is true that the Lord guides individuals, it is also true that He is leading out a people, not just a few separate individuals here and there, with one believing this thing and another that. We know that when Jesus went back to heaven He gave gifts to the church. "He Himself gave some to be apostles, some prophets, some evangelists, and some pastors and teachers, for the equipping of the saints for the work of ministry, for the edifying of the body of Christ, till we all come to the unity of the faith and of the knowledge of the Son of God, to a perfect man, to the measure of the stature of the fullness of Christ" (Eph. 4:11-13).

It is also significant that when Jesus taught His disciples to pray He always used plural pronouns when referring to the ones praying. "In this manner, therefore, pray:

Our Father in heaven,
Hallowed be Your name.
Your kingdom come.
Your will be done
On earth as it is in heaven.
Give *us* this day *our* daily bread.
And forgive *us our* debts,
As *we* forgive *our* debtors.
And do not lead *us* into temptation,
But deliver *us* from the evil one.
For Yours is the kingdom and the
Power and the glory forever. Amen" (Matt. 6:9-13).

Therefore, when we pray for God's guidance we should expect to be guided to His Bible-believing people—the ones who are unified by the gifts of the Spirit.

The Greatest Challenge

It is called the world's highest grave. In the spring

of 1999 an American expedition found the body of the legendary George Mallory, who died attempting to scale Mount Everest on June 8, 1924. Decades before Sir Edmond Hillary made his successful assault on the mountain from the south, George Mallory and Andrew Irvine attempted Everest's north face. Others who had stayed at a camp far below had seen them climbing the Northeast Ridge—and then they vanished into the clouds. They were never again seen alive. Irvine's ice ax was discovered in 1933, and then on May 1, 1999, Mallory's frozen body was found at 27,000 feet. There is no way to be sure whether they made it to the top.

At 29,028 feet (five and a half miles) above sea level, Mount Everest is the world's highest mountain. Many climbers have tried to scale the mountain since the British expeditioners first saw it in the 1850s. Avalanches, crevasses, and strong winds have combined with extreme steepness and thin air to make the climb difficult. Sir Edmund Hillary of New Zealand and Tenzing Norgay, a Nepalese Sherpa tribesman and guide, were the first men to reach the top. They were members of a British expedition led by Sir John Hunt. It left Kathmandu, Nepal, on March 10, 1953, and approached the mountain from its south side— which had been called unclimbable. As the climbers advanced up the slopes, they set up a series of camps, each with fewer members. The last camp, one small tent at 27,900 feet, was established by Hillary and Norgay, who reached the summit on May 29 after more than two months of climbing.

Everest has not been friendly to climbers. More

than 150 climbers are believed to have died on its slopes. In the spring of 1999 the bodies of 17 climbers were discovered at different sites on Everest's north face—all between 27,000 feet and the summit. So near yet so far. The famous 1996 storm on Everest's Southeast Ridge, the one used by Hillary and Norgay, killed five climbers, including two guides in one day!

People say they climb a mountain "because it is there" (in words accredited to George Mallory). But the stakes are much greater in our journey to the City of God. We are not just climbing a mountain—even a challenging mountain, where our life might be at risk. We are seeking eternal life! We are willing to risk everything to obtain the prize. It has been promised to us by our faithful Guide, who knows the way and has promised to help us.

Three Promises

To those who trust Him as their guide the Lord has made many promises that bring us courage and hope. Three quickly come to mind:

1. God has promised to go with us wherever we go (Matt. 28:20).

2. God has promised to supply all our needs (Phil. 4:19).

3. God has promised to give us perfect peace (Isa. 26:3).

By following the counsel in God's Word, the life of Jesus, and the guidance of the Holy Spirit, we can know and keep on the way. God also leads through faithful shepherds—pastors who read, understand,

and follow the Word of God. Any guide who claims to be going to heaven but doesn't use the right Guidebook is a false or blind guide. On such an important journey we can't afford to be sidetracked or travel in the wrong direction. It may be time for a midcourse correction.

CHAPTER FIVE

GOD OUTLINES THE FUTURE

When we look at life through the eye of prophecy we can truly say that we are almost home. Beginning with this chapter we will review some of the Bible's most basic prophecies that shine light on our pathway and illuminate the future.

When we accept the Bible as our guide and begin to search it for direction in life, it becomes quite apparent that there is a line drawn through time from eternity in the past to eternity in the future. Beginning in Genesis and continuing until the present, nearly 6,000 years of time are recorded in the pages of sacred history. The balance of time to the close of the millennium and the re-creation of the earth is a matter of prophetic revelation.

By studying history, we can look back and see the road humanity has traveled, and we can see the road ahead through the eyes of the prophets. This "road" through time on the way to eternity is frequently called in Scripture "the way of the Lord."

There are many roads one could choose to take in life. The Bible urges us to choose the way to eternal life and gives directions on how to find it. This sounds quite simple. In fact, it is not! The reason it is not simple is that the devil puts forth his highest efforts to distract and detour those seeking the way to eternal life. As noted previously, Jesus warns His followers several times in Matthew 24, the end-time chapter, to not be deceived.

Many prophecies that were given centuries ago are now a matter of history. By studying these prophecies we can gain an insight into how God communicates with us and how to interpret prophecies that are yet unfulfilled. An overview of four of the Bible's most significant prophecies allows us to see that God knows the end from the beginning and that the course of history was predicted in the prophetic portions of the Bible. By looking at these prophecies we can see not only the future but also the end-time or the latter days of this world's history.

Only two Bible books are primarily apocalyptic. These two unique books pull back the veil and display the ultimate destiny of mankind. They portray a revelation of God in history and predict the future with amazing accuracy. These two books are Daniel and Revelation. Both Daniel and John were in their later years when they penned their respective works.

Both had since their youth developed a deep and abiding relationship with the God of heaven.

Understanding Daniel is a prerequisite for understanding Revelation. And understanding the first part of Daniel is essential to understanding the last part. Apocalyptic prophecy is progressive; it presupposes an understanding of previous prophecy and of each previous step in the revelation. God never intended that prophecy would be complex. In fact, just the opposite is true. He wants prophecy to be a "revelation" of Himself and His activities on behalf of humankind. However, we are told that "none of the wicked shall understand, but the wise shall understand" (Dan. 12:10). In other words, spiritual things are spiritually discerned. The Bible is its own best interpreter, and by spending time in the Word we will gain understanding.

The Babylonian captivity of Israel was a really low point in the history of God's people. Warned of—predicted—for many years by Jeremiah and other prophets, this experience was devastating for the morale of Israel. Yet in spite of the captivity problems, which were the result of their own course of action, God was with them and prospered the faithful ones.

Because the first chapter of Daniel gives the setting for the book, it cannot be overlooked. It tells the story of four young men—in their late teens only, Jewish captives far from home. Offered the rich and unhealthful foods of the king, the young men asked for simple food. They recognized their bodies as the temple of God. "Daniel purposed in his heart that he would not defile himself with the portion of the king's delicacies, nor with the wine which he drank" (Dan. 1:8). "Give us vegetables to eat and water to drink," he requested (verse 12). During their training period "God gave them knowledge and skill in all literature and wisdom; and Daniel had understanding in all visions and dreams" (verse 17).

At the end of their training period they were personally examined by the king. "And in all matters of wisdom and understanding about which the king examined them, he found them ten times better than all the magicians and astrologers who were in all his realm" (verse 20).

The second chapter of Daniel is fundamental to an understanding of the rest of that book and to the later book of Revelation. In the wisdom of God, Daniel 2 is remarkably pleasant to read and easy to understand. And as is true with the first chapter, its profound message is delivered to us as a story. It is simple enough to tell a child and yet in 45 short verses it lays out the entire course of history from Daniel's day to the second coming of Christ!

We read that the Babylonian king Nebuchadnezzar had a remarkable dream one night. It woke him up, and he couldn't go back to sleep. The Bible says that "his spirit was so troubled that his sleep left him" (verse 1). He then called in all his wise men, or counselors. The Bible calls them "the magicians, the astrologers, the sorcerers, and the Chaldeans" (verse 2). He told them that his dream was very significant but that he couldn't remember it; furthermore, he wanted to know its meaning. The wise men were used to giving interpretations of dreams, but they were powerless to come up with the dream itself. Nebuchadnezzar told them that if they could tell him what he dreamed they would be given gifts, rewards, and great honor. If not, they would be cut in pieces and their houses would be made into ash heaps. One can only imagine the fear that swept over the counselors.

The men made a final appeal. No king or ruler had ever asked his counselors such a thing as this, they said, and no one could do what he was asking them to do—"except the gods, whose dwelling is not with flesh" (verse 11). The king became furious and gave a command to his guards that all the counselors should be destroyed.

Apparently Daniel and his three friends were not in the group before the king, perhaps because of their junior status. When the king's guard came to take Daniel and his companions to the execution, the Bible says that Daniel, with tact and wisdom, asked Arioch, the captain of the king's guard, "Why is the decree from the king so harsh?" Obviously, Daniel was well liked by those who knew him, for Arioch told him the whole story.

Daniel ventured into the king's presence and re-quested time to petition his God to reveal the dream and its interpretation. The king granted the request. Immediately Daniel ran to his house and contacted his three friends, Hananiah, Mishael, and Azariah (their Hebrew names), asking them to join him in prayer "that they might seek mercies from the God of heaven concerning this secret, so that Daniel and his companions might not perish with the rest of the wise men of Babylon" (verse 18).

These young men had confidence in God. He had been with them before. They had turned to Him many times for guidance and protection. Now with contrition of heart they submitted themselves anew to the Judge of the earth, pleading that He would grant them deliverance in this time of special need.

God revealed the secret dream of the king to Daniel in a night vision. No doubt when Daniel woke, he quickly wrote out some notes so he wouldn't forget what he had been told. He offered a prayer, saying, "I thank You and praise You, O God of my fathers; You have given me wisdom and might, and have now made known to me what we asked of You, for You have made known to us the king's demand" (verse 23).

Going to Arioch, Daniel told him, "Don't kill the wise men! Take me to the king and I will give him the interpretation." The Bible says that "then Arioch quickly brought Daniel before the king, and said thus to him [apparently taking a little credit to himself], 'I have found a man of the captives of Judah, who will make known to the king the interpretation'" (verse 25).

There stood Daniel, the Jewish captive, courteous, calm, and self-possessed. The king, perhaps remembering this outstanding student he had examined earlier, asked, "Are you able to make known to me the dream which I have seen, and its interpretation?" (verse 26).

Daniel could have just said, "Yes." But he didn't. Instead he gave a little preface to his answer. He said that what the king had asked of his wise men they couldn't answer. "But there is a God in heaven who reveals secrets, and He has made known to King Nebuchadnezzar what will be in the latter days" (verse 28). Here is an indication that God wants us to know about future events and the last days!

Then Daniel began to tell the dream. You can be sure that everyone in the room, especially the king, was listening closely.

"You, O king, were watching; and behold, a great image! This great image, whose splendor was excellent, stood before you; and its form was awesome" (verse 31). The king moved to the edge of his throne and exclaimed, "That's it! You've got it! Go on!"

Daniel continued, "This image's head was of fine gold, its chest and arms of silver, its belly and thighs of bronze, its legs of iron, its feet partly of iron and partly of clay. You watched while a stone was cut out without hands, which struck the image on its feet of iron and clay, and broke them in pieces. Then the iron, the clay, the bronze, the silver, and the gold were crushed together, and became like chaff from the summer threshing floors; the wind carried them away so that no trace of them was found. And the stone that struck the image became a great mountain and filled the whole earth" (verses 32-35).

I can imagine the king, forgetting royal protocol, springing to his feet and hugging Daniel and saying, "You are exactly right, young man. Now, what does it mean?" Since he knows it was the very dream that had troubled him, he's receptive to its interpretation. Daniel responds, "Now we [apparently including his three friends, as is later evident] will tell the interpretation of it before the king" (verse 36).

The interpretation, recorded in your Bible, is a model of clarity. The Bible interprets itself—it is indeed simple!

The Interpretation

The king sits back down, and Daniel continues, "You, O king, are a king of kings. For the God of heaven has given you a kingdom, power, strength, and glory; and wherever the children of men dwell, or the beasts of the field and the birds of the heaven, He has given them into your hand, and has made you ruler over them all—you are this head of gold" (verses 37, 38).

The king of Babylon rules a vast empire. But is the head of gold referring to the king himself or to his kingdom? The next verse gives the answer.

"But after you shall arise another kingdom [not another "king"] inferior to yours; then another, a third kingdom of bronze, which shall rule over all the earth" (verse 39). Please note that these successive kingdoms "rule over all the earth." They are world empires in the sense that they rule over all the earth known to the people of God. But Daniel is not finished yet.

"And the fourth kingdom shall be as strong as iron, inasmuch as iron breaks in pieces and shatters everything; and like iron that crushes, that kingdom will break in pieces and crush all the others. Whereas you saw the feet and toes, partly of potter's clay and partly of iron, the kingdom shall be divided; yet the strength of the iron shall be in it, just as you saw the iron mixed with ceramic clay. And as the toes of the feet were partly of iron and partly of clay, so the kingdom shall be partly strong and partly fragile. As you saw iron mixed with ceramic clay, they will mingle with the seed of men; but they will not adhere to one another, just as iron does not mix with clay. And in the days of these kings [following the division of the fourth empire] the God of heaven will set up a kingdom which shall never be destroyed; and the kingdom shall not be left to other people; it shall break in pieces and consume all these kingdoms, and it shall stand forever" (verses 40-44).

The bottom line is simple. There would be four great empires beginning with Babylon—only four. Four empires would make significant impact on God's chosen people. The fourth one would not be conquered as the first three were by a succeeding great empire, but it would be "divided," or broken up among various "kings." Oh yes, many leaders would try to make another empire in the areas covered by the four, but their attempts would fail.

Daniel concludes the interpretation for King Nebuchadnezzar by saying, "Inasmuch as you saw that the stone was cut out of the mountain without hands, and that it broke in pieces the iron, the bronze, the clay, the silver, and the gold—the great God has made known to the king what will come to pass after this. The dream is certain, and its interpretation is sure" (verse 45). Daniel is confident of the dream and its interpretation because he is confident in God!

Picture the scene in the king's royal quarters. The king prostrates himself before Daniel (verse 46) and commands that they should present an offering and incense to him. The king tells Daniel that his God is the God of gods, and truly the Lord is a revealer of secrets—"since you could reveal this secret" (verse 47).

The king gives Daniel many great gifts and made him ruler over the whole province of Babylon and the chief administrator of the wise men. Daniel, in his greatness and humility, petitions the king on behalf of his three friends, and they are given positions of leadership as well.

Sometimes in a study of history it appears that events were shaped because of the strength or prowess of human beings, but this prophecy reveals the hand and wisdom of God. Before these empires came upon the stage of action, God looked down the ages and predicted their rise and fall. Bible students have not always been able to interpret prophecies accurately in advance, but when we look back we can see their fulfillment—and that gives us confidence in the God of prophecy.

Daniel lived long enough to see the beginning of the second empire of the king's dream. Among Nebuchadnezzar's successors were Nabonidus and Belshazzar. The latter put on a feast, and the elder statesman was summoned to come to it to render another interpretation—the handwriting on the wall! Daniel's last words to this king were "Your kingdom has been divided, and given to the Medes and Persians" (Dan. 5:28).

The prophet Ezra confirms this in the words of the Persian king: "Thus says Cyrus king of Persia: All the kingdoms of the earth the Lord God of heaven has given me" (Ezra 1:2).

Later through a "heavenly messenger" God revealed to Daniel the identity of the third empire as well! The messenger asked, "Do you know why I have come to you? And now I must return to fight with the prince of Persia; and when I have gone forth, indeed the prince of Greece will come" (Dan. 10:20).

Three out of four is not bad. Do you think the Bible also reveals the identity of the fourth empire? Yes, it does—in the New Testament! In Luke 2:1 we learn that Caesar Augustus issued a decree that "all the world" should be registered for tax purposes. Who was Caesar Augustus? A Roman emperor. So Rome was the fourth kingdom. The legs of iron in Nebuchadnezzar's dream could represent no other kingdom, because Rome was the only universal kingdom that came to power after Greece. So when Jesus appeared among human beings almost 2,000 years ago the course of history had already reached the legs of iron.

C. Mervyn Maxwell, in his excellent two-volume work on Daniel and the Revelation, *God Cares,* summarizes the sequence this way: "After he [Nebuchadnezzar] died in 562 B.C. the Babylonian Empire ran rapidly downhill. Media and Persia, powers inferior to Babylon during Nebuchadnezzar's lifetime, were united together and linked to Lydia by Cyrus, king of Persia. They conquered Babylon in 539 B.C.

"The Medo-Persian Empire continued for a while to expand in wealth, power, and size (adding Egypt); but like Babylon, it too went into decline. In 331 B.C. it was vanquished by Alexander the Great, founder of the Macedonian Greek Empire. At Alexander's death his dominion was divided into a number of

Hellenistic Greek kingdoms. Meanwhile Rome was evolving in the west and, in due course, began to influence the Hellenistic kingdoms. By 168 B.C. Rome dominated the Mediterranean as the fourth empire of the statue prophecy.

"Babylonian, Medo-Persian, Greek, Roman—the list of empires is simple and can be memorized in a moment. Any good history book will confirm the sequence" (C. M. Maxwell, *God Cares* [Nampa, Idaho: Pacific Press], vol. 1, pp. 35, 36).

Daniel 2 is foundational. It is basic to understanding all prophecy that follows it chronologically. It provides the structure upon which one can add the additional details from other prophecies regarding these same and subsequent players in human history.

The Bible's own interpretation is sure. And a basic truth of Daniel 2 is that all of the major elements but the second coming of Christ are already written in the history books! We are indeed living in those "later times" spoken of by Daniel. We are almost home!

CHAPTER SIX

NATIONS COME AND GO

In the previous chapter we noted that Daniel 2 gives us the basic structure of world history right down to the second coming of Christ. In fact, by the time of Christ's first advent history had already reached the time of the fourth and final "world empire." So what about all the time between then and now? Do we have any indication from Bible prophecy what we should expect in those intervening years? Certainly. God wants us to know what is happening and what we may expect in the future.

Daniel 7 covers the same basic time period as Daniel 2, and therefore the same nations are the players, but we are given much greater detail. Also, information is given that fills in the great time gap after the fall of Rome. This chapter is a wonderful valida-tion of the truth that amidst the strife and tumult of nations God still has the final say in the affairs of the earth. He knows what is going on!

Daniel 7 begins with a date: "the first year of Belshazzar king of Babylon." This helps us to pin-point the time of the vision. Historians tell us that Nebuchadnezzar was succeeded on the Babylonian throne by Nabonidus, who "entrusted the kingship" to Belshazzar in 553 B.C.—the date of this vision.

The chapters of the book of Daniel, like that of Revelation, are not all arranged chronologically. As chapter 7 opens, Nebuchadnezzar has been dead for nine years and things aren't going very well for Babylon. Daniel is no longer a young man. He is about 70 now, though apparently not fully retired. The fall of Babylon described in chapter 5 and Daniel's experience in the lions' den of chapter 6 are still in the future. Fifty years or so have passed since the vision of Daniel 2. No doubt that experience is still vivid in the mind of Daniel.

Then we read that "Daniel had a dream and vi-sions of his head while on his bed" (Dan. 7:1). He writes down the dream, making an outline of the main facts. He sees that "the four winds of heaven were stir-ring up the Great Sea. And four great beasts came up from the sea, each different from the other. The first was like a lion, and had eagle's wings. I watched till its wings were plucked off; and it was lifted up from the earth and made to stand on two feet like a man, and a man's heart was given to it. And suddenly an-other beast, a second, like a bear. It was raised up on one side, and had three ribs in its mouth between its teeth. And they said to it: 'Arise, devour much flesh!' After this I looked, and there was another, like a leopard, which had on its back four wings of a bird. The beast had four heads, and dominion was given to it. After this I saw in the night visions, and behold a fourth beast, dreadful and terrible, exceedingly strong. It had huge iron teeth; it was devouring, breaking in pieces, and trampling the residue with its feet. It was different from all the beasts that were before it, and it had ten horns" (verses 2-7).

Then Daniel observes a unique feature in the dream—a little horn. This little horn is really the focus of this chapter because it describes something not mentioned in the empire progression of Daniel 2. Daniel puts it this way:

"I was considering the horns, and there was another horn, a little one, coming up among them, before whom three of the first horns were plucked out by the roots. And there, in this horn, were eyes like the eyes of a man, and a mouth speaking pompous words" (verse 8).

Daniel continues to watch the portrayal until he is shown the awesome view of a heavenly judgment where "the Ancient of Days was seated. . . . The court was seated, and the books were opened" (verses 9, 10). Then he is apparently distracted by the sounds of the little horn.

"I watched then because of the sound of the pompous words which the horn was speaking; I watched till the beast was slain, and its body destroyed and given to the burning flame. As for the rest of the beasts, they had their dominion taken away, yet their lives were prolonged for a season and a time" (verses 11, 12).

In his account Daniel says that he was next given a view of the second coming of the Son of Man and the setting up of His kingdom, "which shall not pass away" (verse 14). But the vision troubles him, and he wants a better understanding of what it means. He is particularly concerned about the fourth beast with its 10 horns, and curious about its "little horn." Daniel states that he came near to "one of those who stood by." We may assume that it was an angel, a heavenly messenger. He asks the angel "the truth of all this" (verse 16).

The Interpretation

God clearly wants us to understand prophecy. He does not want us to be in darkness. Immediately He provided an interpretation to Daniel through the angel. "So he told me and made known to me the interpretation" (verse 16). The angel first gives Daniel a short summary:

"Those great beasts, which are four, are four kings which arise out of the earth. But the saints of the Most High shall receive the kingdom, and possess the kingdom forever, even forever and ever."

Just two sentences. That's all Daniel is given until he asks for more. But surely the angel wants Daniel to see the similarity with the vision of chapter 2—the vision of the metallic image. There will be four kingdoms, and then God's everlasting kingdom. But Daniel isn't satisfied with that simple explanation. He wants to know more about the fourth beast and its horns and the strange "little horn." And so the Bible record continues:

"Thus he [the angel] said: 'The fourth beast shall be a fourth kingdom on the earth, which shall be different from all other kingdoms, and shall devour the whole earth, trample it and break it in pieces' " (verse 23). Knowing that the fourth beast is the fourth kingdom, we recognize at once that we are seeing the same series of world powers that we discussed in the previous chapter while reviewing Daniel 2: Babylonian, Medo-Persian, Greek, and Roman empires, followed in due time by the kingdom of God. But now more details are given.

The angel continues his interpretation: "The ten horns are ten kings who shall arise from this kingdom. And another shall rise after them; he shall be different from the first ones, and shall subdue three kings. He shall speak pompous words against the Most High, shall persecute the saints of the Most High, and shall intend to change times and law. Then the saints shall be given into his hand for a time and times and half a time" (verses 24, 25).

The angel's interpretation of the mysterious little horn clearly helps to identify it as the powerful church-state of the Middle Ages—papal Rome, later to be known as the Roman Catholic Church. For a positive identification let's review the clues given by the angel.

1. Location. The little horn arose out of the fourth beast. It came up among the 10 horns (nations) of western Europe into which the civil or pagan

Roman Empire was divided (verses 8, 24). Did papal Rome originate within the territory of the old Roman Empire? Yes.

2. Time of rise. It appeared after the 10 other horns, that is, after the breakup of the Roman Empire, which culminated during the sixth century A.D. Further, it would rise after three of the horns (kings) had been uprooted (verses 8, 20, 24).

The church founded by Christ and the apostles existed from the first century, but papal domination did not begin until after the fall of the Roman Empire. Did papal Rome arise after the fifth century? Yes. Three of the barbarian powers that featured in the breakup of the Roman Empire espoused the views of Arius, who denied the divinity of Christ. All the other barbarian kingdoms came to accept the Christian faith. From A.D. 476 on, the three Arian powers dominated portions of the territory of Rome, but each in turn met defeat as the rulers of the Eastern Roman Empire rallied to support the Roman Church in the west.

In 533 Justinian, the emperor of the Eastern Empire, officially recognized the bishop (later to be called pope) of Rome as the head of all the Christian churches. But because of the Arian domination of Rome, the pope had no opportunity to actually exercise this authority. Five years later, in 538, Belisarius, one of Justinian's generals, routed the Ostrogoths, the last of the Arian powers, from the city of Rome. So by the military intervention of the Eastern Empire the pope was freed from the dominating influence of states that restrained his activities in the civil sphere. This date, A.D. 538, plays a significant part in another clue that helps to identify the little horn as the Papacy.

3. The nature of the little horn. It was different from the other horns, and though it was little at first, it became "greater than his fellows" (verses 8, 20, 24). Was papal Rome different than the other kingdoms that emerged from the Roman Empire? Yes indeed. While the other powers were political entities, the Papacy was both political and religious in nature.

4. Rise to power. It would "subdue three kings" or pluck them up "by the roots" (verses 24, 8). Did papal Rome uproot three kingdoms as it came to power? Yes. As mentioned above, three of the 10 kingdoms that emerged from the ashes of pagan Rome were Arian in religious thinking. These were the Heruli, the Vandals, and the Ostrogoths. They were, with the aid of the Eastern Empire, defeated by papal Rome, allowing it more dominant control. These three kingdoms have no modern counterparts.

5. Attitude toward God. The little horn would "speak pompous words against the Most High" (verse 25). What does this mean? It is generally understood among Bible scholars that speaking against the Most High is equivalent to taking on the prerogatives of God and/or blaspheming His name. Much could be written on this topic. The following should be sufficient to make the point of identification.

"The admission that the 'teaching authority of the Roman Church' is vested in men of unequal virtue and competence contrasts with a claim made as recently as the 1890s by Pope Leo XIII. In an encyclical letter, 'On the Chief Duties of Christians as Citizens,' dated January 10, 1890, Leo XIII asserted that 'the supreme teacher in the Church is the Roman Pontiff. Union of minds, therefore, requires . . . complete submission and obedience of will to the Church and to the Roman Pontiff, *as to God Himself.'* On June 20, 1894, in 'The Reunion of Christendom,' Leo claimed further that 'we [that is, himself, as the other popes] hold upon this earth the place of God Almighty'" (C. M. Maxwell, *God Cares,* vol. 1, p. 131).

Does papal Rome claim the prerogatives of God? Yes.

6. **Attitude toward God's people**. The little horn was to persecute or "wear out the saints of the Most High" (verse 25, KJV). According to the angel's interpretation to Daniel this power would persecute God's people. Those whom papal Rome considered heretical faced civil punishment. History attests that millions were put to death under this religiopolitical system. For a firsthand look, visit the archbishop's fortress in Salzburg, Austria. For a period of more than 400 years Salsburg was a city-state and the archbishop was also the king. Take the guided tour of the fortress and see the torture chamber where enemies of the archbishop and "heretics" were tortured until they "confessed" and then were executed.

Did papal Rome persecute the saints? Yes. In fact, a special closed-door symposium called by Pope John Paul II convened on October 23-28, 1998, to discuss the Inquisition, which was the church's mechanism for investigating suspected heretics; it operated from the thirteenth to the nineteenth centuries. At the symposium a Vatican-issued background paper addressed questions such as the extent to which the Inquisition employed torture, and the number of suspected heretics who were put to death.

"Calling the Inquisition 'a tormented phase of Church history,' Pope John Paul II said that studying this history can teach the Church how 'methods of intolerance and even violence in the service of the truth' fall short of the Gospel.

"The Pope is scheduled to pronounce a 'request for forgiveness' on Ash Wednesday in the year 2000, a statement expected to address the Inquisition and other dark moments in the Church's history" (*Our Sunday Visitor,* Nov. 15, 1998, p. 4).

7. Attitude toward God's law. The little horn would attempt or "think" to change times and laws (verse 25, KJV). It would view God's law as needing changes and would attempt to make changes in that law by its own authority. Several examples will illustrate this. Many could be given. Significantly, the Roman Catholic Church does not adhere to the basic Protestant notion that the Bible and the Bible only should be the standard of faith and practice. There are three major "sources of truth" for the Roman Catholic: the Bible, tradition, and the "magisterium," or the teaching authority of the church, which includes, of course, the excathedra words of the pope.

Here is an example of the church's statements:

"At the great Council of Trent (1545-1563), convened by the pope to stanch the onrush of Protestantism, Gaspare de Fosso, the archbishop of Reggio, in an address of January 18, 1562, brought the issue up again. 'The authority of the church,' said he, 'is illustrated most clearly by the Scriptures; for while on the one hand she [the church] recommends them, declares them to be divine, [and] offers them to us to be read, . . . on the other hand, the legal precepts in the Scriptures taught by the Lord have ceased by virtue of the same authority [the church]. The Sabbath, the most glorious day in the law, has been changed into the Lord's day. . . . These and other similar matters have not ceased by virtue of Christ's teaching (for He says He has come to fulfill the law, not to destroy it), but they have been changed by the authority of the church'" (Maxwell, *God Cares,* vol. 1, p. 134).

Hundreds of years later the Roman Church still asserts she can change God's law. Recently I purchased two books from a Catholic organization, Our Lady's Book Service, operated by the Servants of Jesus and Mary in Constable, New York. Both books have the imprimatur or blessing of the church. One book, by the renowned James Cardinal Gibbons, archbishop of Baltimore, states: "The scriptures alone do not contain all the truths which a Christian is obliged to practice. Not to mention other examples, is not every Christian obligated to sanctify Sunday and to abstain on that day from unnecessary servile work? Is not the observance of this law among the most prominent of our sacred duties? *But you may read the Bible from Genesis to Revelation, and you will not find a single line authorizing the sanctification of Sunday. The Scriptures enforce the religious observance of Saturday, a day which we never sanctify"* (Gibbons, *The Faith of Our Fathers* [reprinted by TAN Books and Publishers, 1980], pp. 72, 73, 1876; italics supplied).

The other book is Peter Geiermann's catechism. His comments, in question-and-answer format, on the Sabbath commandment are as follows:

"Q. *What is the Third Commandment?* [Note: Catholics place the Sabbath command third.]

"A. The Third Commandment is: Remember that thou keep holy the Sabbath day.

"Q. *Which is the Sabbath day?*

"A. Saturday is the Sabbath day.

"Q. *Why do we observe Sunday instead of Saturday?*

"A. We observe Sunday instead of Saturday because the Catholic Church transferred the solemnity from Saturday to Sunday" (Rev. Peter Geiermann, C.S.S.R., *The Convert's Catechism of Catholic Doctrine,* p. 50).

In addition, in Catholic listings of the Ten Commandments the second commandment is dropped altogether. Many of the others have been abbreviated, robbing them of their full meaning. The tenth is divided in order to make a total of 10. In the comments on the fourth commandment (called the third) in the new catechism, paragraph 2190, states: *"The sabbath,* which represented the completion of the first creation, *has been replaced by Sunday,* which recalls the new creation inaugurated by the Resurrection of Christ" (*The Catechism of the Catholic Church* [1994], p. 529; italics supplied).

Did papal Rome try to change God's law? Yes.

8. Length of time permitted to rule. The power represented by the little horn was to rule for "a time and times and half a time" (verse 25). Again, this is not complicated. A "time" in Daniel is a year (see the Septuagint version of this passage), or 360 days in prophecy. "Times" would be two years or 720 days, and half a time would be 180 days. Add them up and you get 1,260 days. This harmonizes with Revelation 13:5, in which this period is spoken of as 42 months (42 months x 30 days per month = 1,260 days), and in Revelation 12:6, where the figure given is 1,260 days—all referring to the same period.

Remember that we are dealing here with symbols. The beasts, the horns—all are symbols. So it is not surprising that time should be expressed in symbol as well. Ezekiel 4:6 gives an example of Bible time prophecy—a day in prophetic time equals a year in literal time.

Remember, as we noted in item 2 above (time of the rise to power), that the Roman Catholic Church came to power in A.D. 538 . Adding the 1,260 years of time it was given to rule brings us to 1798. It so happened that in 1798, 1,260 years after 538, the French general Berthier, under the direction of the military government of France, arrested Pope Pius VI in Rome and took him captive to France, where he ultimately died in exile.

Did papal Rome dominate Europe during the 1,260-year period from 538 to 1798? Yes.

These eight identifying characteristics of the "little horn" clearly point to the Roman Catholic Church. What other power, different than the other nations, arose after the fall of the Roman Empire from among the divided kingdoms, destroyed three of the kingdoms, spoke blasphemy against God, persecuted

God's saints, tried to change God's law, and dominated Europe for 1,260 years? None but the Roman Catholic Church. No other power or entity even comes close to meeting the conditions. The little horn power is quite obviously the Roman Catholic Church.

But this takes us only to 1798. Does God leave us there to wonder what will happen next? Not at all. Remember that prophecy is progressive and builds on what happens or is given before. In order to fill in the prophetic picture right up to the turn of the millennium we go to the apocalyptic book of Revelation. God gave the apostle John the same view of the future that He gave Daniel. However, by the time of John the first three world empires were already history he was living during the fourth and final world empire. Summarizing what had been given before, God quickly brings John up to speed in an impressive vision.

"Then I stood on the sand of the sea. And I saw a beast rising up out of the sea, having seven heads and ten horns, and on his horns ten crowns, and on his heads a blasphemous name. Now the beast which I saw was like a leopard, his feet were like the feet of a bear, and his mouth like the mouth of a lion. The dragon gave him his power, his throne, and great authority" (Rev. 13:1, 2).

This beast rises up out of the sea, which represents a populated area (Rev. 17:15). John sees a unique symbol—a beast with the body of a leopard, the feet of a bear, and the mouth of a lion. These are the same animals of Daniel 7. In his vision Daniel saw a lion (symbolizing Babylon), a bear (Medo-Persia), a leopard (Greece), and finally a "dreadful and terrible" beast (Rome). According to his vision, the fourth empire, Rome, would come to be dominated in its final stage by a "little horn," a terrible power that would persecute God's people for "a time and times and half a time."

John's vision and prophecy is similar to the description of the little horn in Daniel 7; it unquestionably points to the time when the apostate papal church system of the Middle Ages began to dominate the state. The apostle Paul referred to this power as the "man of sin," and the "mystery of lawlessness" (see 2 Thess. 2:3, 7).

One aspect of Revelation 13 is most significant. After ruling for 1,260 years, through the Middle Ages and until 1798, the Papacy appeared to receive a deadly wound. But this chapter in Revelation reveals an additional fact. The deadly wound heals and all the world marvels and follows the beast (Rev. 13:3). Evidently the Papacy will play a major role in end-time events.

In identifying the role of the Papacy and Roman Catholicism, I want to emphasize that I have no bone to pick with Catholic people. Without question there are many wonderful, God-fearing individuals in the Roman Catholic Church. The Bible is quite clear on that (Rev. 14:7; 18:4). God does not condemn these people. Rather, it is the *system* to which God objects—the mingling of church and state, or as Revelation 17:1 shows, the prostitution of the church to the state.

The bottom line here is simple and straightforward. In the outline of prophecy as given in the books of Daniel and the Revelation, papal Rome as a system is a major player. One can logically draw no other conclusion. We note that God showed, progressively to three different people—King Nebuchadnezzar, the prophet Daniel, and John the revelator, that there would be four world empires, that the fourth empire would be divided up into smaller nations, that a different kind of power with civil and religious powers would rule from 538 to 1798 and then receive a deadly wound, which would later be healed and receive the honor and recognition of the world.

As we study the testimony of this prophetic picture we can see that history has validated these predictions with uncanny accuracy. But there is more detail that helps us to see that we are indeed nearing the end of this world's history.

CHAPTER SEVEN

WORLD SUPERPOWER

Suppose you were traveling a road with which you were unacquainted. You inquire of a stranger, who tells you that the road leads to a glorious city, filled with every good thing, governed by the most lovely, mild, and benevolent prince that the world has ever seen. In that city there is neither sickness, sorrow, pain, nor death. He then tells you what you may expect to pass on the road—landmarks by which you may know that he has told you the truth, and which will mark the progress you have made.

First, he tells you, you will come to a monument that can be seen from a great distance; on the top of it you will see a lion with eagle's wings. At some distance beyond that, you will come to another monument, upon which is a bear with three ribs in its mouth. Passing farther on, you will at length arrive at a monument on the top of which you will see a leopard with four wings and four heads. After that you will come to a fourth monument, upon which is a beast like none you have ever seen or heard of. It looks dreadful and terrible, with great iron teeth, and instead of the usual two horns it has 10. Finally you will come to a monument that has upon it the same unusual beast as the previous one but with this difference: three of the 10 horns of the beast have been removed and in their place is a very unusual horn that has many strange characteristics.

Are you beginning to get the picture? This journey is the one described in the Bible in the seventh chapter of Daniel. As you remember, the beasts represent nations that have played major roles in relation to God's people down through the ages. Now we are nearing the end of the journey. We are almost home. We can see the lights of the city.

Many nations have played important parts in history. However, only a relatively small number actually play a major role in Bible prophecy and salvation history. They are Babylon, Medo-Persia, Greece, Rome, the Papacy, and, as we shall see, the United States of America. There are many explicit characteristics of the United States that help to identify it as the last great earthly power to play a role in salvation history.

Daniel was promised by an angel that his book, though it would be sealed for a period of time, would be opened and understood at the time of the end (see Dan. 12:4, 9, 10). Revelation, on the other hand, was to be just that—a revelation of Jesus Christ that would show His servants things "which must shortly take place" (Rev. 1:1; 22:6). On the other hand, when we use our own human speculation regarding prophetic interpretation instead of letting the Bible be its own interpreter, we come up with all kinds of weird interpretations. Remember, God wants us to know.

For years many Christians have understood that the second beast mentioned in Revelation 13:11, the beast that arose from the land rather than the sea, the beast with horns like a lamb, is the United States of America. The reason it is important to identify the power represented by this beast is that it eventually cooperates with the revived or "healed" Papacy at the end of time. These two will be the final players in the great drama of the ages.

In the previous chapter we noted that apparently when God gave John his vision in Revelation 13 He took it for granted that His servant John would be familiar with the book of Daniel and its beasts in chapter 7. So basically Revelation 13 does not go all the way back to Babylon and move systematically forward as Daniel 2 and 7 do. Instead, the vision of Revelation 13 makes a quick two-verse summary to bring John up to speed and then proceeds to give more details that help to make a positive identification of the little horn power.

But now another beast *rises out of the earth.* "He had two horns like a lamb and spoke like a dragon" (Rev. 13: 11). Again the biblical clues give unmistakable evidence as to its identity. Here are some of the identifying characteristics of this beast with horns like a lamb:

1. It arises about the time when the first beast, the Papacy, is wounded (verses 3, 11).

2. Unlike the first beast of Revelation 13 and the beasts of Daniel 7, it comes up out of the earth (verse 11).

3. It has two horns like a lamb (verse 11).

4. It speaks like a dragon (verse 11).

5. It has a worldwide influence (verses 12, 14).

6. It has authority like the first beast (verse 12).

7. It supports the first beast (verses 14, 15).

8. It encourages worship of the first beast (verse 15)

9. It performs great signs (verses 13, 14).

10. It becomes a persecuting power (verses 15, 17).

11. It causes many to receive the mark of the first beast (verse 16).

In apocalyptic symbolism beasts represent kings or kingdoms. Accordingly, we can begin by looking for a kingdom or nation that fits the clues given in Revelation 13. It is an almost inescapable conclusion that the clues point to the United States of America. The clues reveal:

1. The time of its rise to power. We should look for a country that is rising to power around 1798, the time when the Papacy received its "deadly wound." The Pilgrims landed in the New World in the early 1600s. The various settlements known as colonies slowly began to bond together during the 1600s and 1700s. In 1776 the American colonies unified to the point that the Declaration of Independence was drawn up. In 1787 the Constitution was framed, and in 1789 the Bill of Rights was formulated. In 1791 the Bill of Rights was adopted. As we noted in the previous chapter, it was a French general (Berthier) who took the pope captive in 1798, and it is no doubt significant that in that same year the French government recognized the United States as a nation.

2. The geographic area of the new nation. All the other beasts or kingdoms in the prophetic lineup rose from the sea, which as we have seen from Revelation 17:15 represents "peoples, multitudes, nations, and tongues." The other nations we have been studying came to power amid the peoples of the earth by conquering them. Babylon conquered its surrounding nations, including Israel; Medo-Persia conquered Babylon, etc.; but this beast came up "out of the earth." So the nation we are looking for is one that "developed" or "grew up" by exploration, colonization, and development, not by conquest.

The North American continent was colonized by people moving here from other nations. Literally millions came to America from England, France, Ireland, Italy, Germany, and other countries of Europe initially, and then from all parts of the world. Who hasn't heard of Ellis Island and the Statue of Liberty? On the base of the Statue of Liberty are these lines from a poem by Emma Lazarus:

"Give me your tired, your poor,
Your huddled masses yearning to breathe free,
The wretched refuse of your teeming shore,
Send these, the homeless, tempest-tost to me,
I lift my lamp beside the golden door!"

And still today they want to come! The idea called by many the "American experiment" lies at the core of American history. But it was not without a struggle. There was a great civil war: Americans fighting Americans over differences in ideology.

Just a little farther than an hour's drive from my home is the little community of Gettysburg, Pennsylvania. The battle fought there July 1-3, 1863, marked a turning point in that war. In a dedication ceremony for a cemetery for those slain there, President Abraham Lincoln began his famous Gettysburg Address with these words: "Four score and seven years ago our fathers brought forth on this continent, a new nation, conceived in liberty, and dedicated to the proposition that all men are created equal."

The Emma Lazarus poem on the Statue of Liberty and Lincoln's Gettysburg Address show that from a simply historical perspective the United States is truly a "new nation." There can be no question that the United States fits the second clue.

3. It has two horns like a lamb. Some Bible commentators refer to this beast as the lamblike beast. The Bible doesn't call the beast lamblike. The beast grows to be big and powerful, but it has "lamblike" horns. Maybe a bison—which some have pictured—would be more like the beast that John saw. What do the two horns represent? I believe they could quite logically represent the "gentle" characteristics of civil and religious liberty—politically, no king; religiously, no authoritarian pope.

4. It becomes very powerful. Revelation says it "spoke like a dragon." The United States is the only remaining world superpower today. No country on earth has the political or military muscle of the United States. Yet this clue is only partially fulfilled at present. We may expect to see it further fulfilled in the near future.

Satan is referred to as the "dragon" (Rev. 12:9). But Satan also works through the other dragon-like beasts of prophecy. So apparently the United States will become more Satan-like near the end. Some might wonder how the United States could ever "speak as a dragon" and become a persecuting power. But stranger things have happened.

The founders of the United States wisely sought to guard against the entanglement of secular and religious powers, with its inevitable result—intolerance and persecution. The Constitution provides that "Congress shall make no law respecting an establishment of religion, or prohibiting the free exercise thereof" and that "no religious test shall ever be required as a qualification to any office of public trust under the United States." Only in flagrant violation of these safeguards to the nation's liberty can any religious observance be enforced by civil authority. But as unlikely as this may seem, the biblical symbolism indicates that it will be so. The Bible says that this beast with horns like a lamb—apparently gentle in spirit—will speak as a dragon.

5. It has worldwide influence. With the demise of the former Soviet Union the United States leads the world. For example, the success of Operation Desert Storm was possible only with the power and technology of the United States.

This worldwide influence was recognized by Malachi Martin in *The Keys of This Blood,* published in 1990. In the introduction to his book Martin says that there was a three-way struggle for world dominion between the pope (Roman Catholicism), Gorbachev (the Soviet Union), and the capitalist West (the United States and its allies). Martin expects the pope to be the victor in the struggle and that "those of us under seventy will see at least the basic structures of the new world government installed" (pp. 15, 16). He continues: "It is not too much to say, in fact, that the chosen purpose of John Paul's pontificate—the engine that drives his papal grand policy and that determines his day-to-day, year-by-year strategies—is to be the victor in that competition, now well under way" (p. 17).

There can be no question that the United States does have worldwide influence today.

6. It exercises all the authority of the first beast. The chief characteristic of the first beast is that it enforces religious tenets with civil power. Even now in America there are forces seeking to bring about this type of situation, in violation of both the letter and the spirit of the Constitution.

7. It supports and encourages worship of the first beast. President Ronald Reagan established full diplomatic relations with the central government of the Roman Catholic Church, the only church so recognized. Further, the word "worship" seems to indicate religious affiliation as well as political. We note that religious figures such as Chuck Colson, Pat Robertson, Billy Graham, and others encourage support of Rome. Top political leaders are giving support to the aims of Rome.

9. It performs great signs. Revelation 13 mentions such signs as "fire coming down from heaven" (verse 13). Significantly, this type of sign is now being predicted by "the Blessed Virgin Mother, Mary," in apparitions around the world.

10. **It becomes a persecuting power**. This characteristic of the beast with lamblike horns has yet to be revealed. But as history bears out, whenever church and state join hands intolerance and persecution always follow.

11. It causes many to receive the mark of the beast. The United States, founded on the principles of civil and religious liberty and blessed of God, will be instrumental in bringing about the mark of the beast.

Taken together, these clues are very clear. They point unmistakably to the United States as the second beast of Revelation 13—the beast with lamblike horns.

In this chapter and the previous two chapters we have noted that Bible prophecies indicate that after the great world empires, when political powers would be fragmented, the Papacy would rise to dominance and then receive an apparently deadly wound but survive. The United States would rise to prominence and grow into a mighty power. Then these two powers would begin to cooperate with each other. We see this happening before our very eyes! We are witnessing the uncanny accuracy of the prophetic guide.

As I mentioned earlier, there are two major factors that let us know where we are in time. They are (1) the prophecies that point out the rise and fall of nations and (2) the signs of the end—the conditions in the world that will exist at the end of time. We will look at the unmistakable signs of the end in the next chapter.

CHAPTER EIGHT

SIGNS OF THE END

s we have noted, the Bible outlines the course of history in advance through its great prophecies. The great world empires have come and gone. The final players have taken center stage. But in addition to the prophetic time line to guide thoughtful students to a knowledge of where we are in time, God has given us a second tracking system that confirms and fine-tunes our prophetic position. This second system is called God's waymarks, or signs of the end. These signs or end-time indicators are given in both the Old Testament and the New Testament, and they are having a remarkable fulfillment in our time. We will be able to review only a limited number because of the size constraints of this book; however, it is clear that we are seeing God-given signs every bit as significant as when the animals entered the ark in the days of Noah.

When the Major Signs Will Begin

Jesus told His disciples, "Immediately after the tribulation of those days the sun will be darkened, and the moon will not give its light; the stars will fall from heaven, and the powers of the heavens will be shaken. Then the sign of the Son of Man will appear in heaven, and then all the tribes of the earth will mourn, and they will see the Son of Man coming on the clouds of heaven with power and great glory" (Matt. 24:29, 30). John the revelator also predicted these astral phenomena, and stated that a great earthquake would precede them (Rev. 6:12). All of these events would occur some time around the end of the 1,260 years of persecution (Rev. 6) and mark the beginning of the time of the end.

On November 1, 1755, the largest earthquake recorded on earth struck Lisbon, Portugal. Its effects were observed in Europe, Africa, and America, covering an area of nearly 4 million square miles. In Lisbon public and private buildings were leveled and thousands of people were killed. Many people who survived the quake recognized it as a prophetic sign of the end and many gave serious consideration to the judgment of God and began studying prophecy.

Twenty-five years after the great earthquake there occurred the first of the phenomena mentioned by Jesus, the darkening of the sun and moon. On May 19, 1780, an unusual darkness descended upon the northeastern part of the North American continent. Many leading men of the day wrote down their impressions of the great darkness. Timothy Dwight, president of Yale University, noted that candles were lighted in many homes; birds became silent and disappeared, and chickens went to their roosts. It was generally believed that the day of judgment was near.

Observers reported that the thick darkness persisted until after midnight and when the moon became visible it had the appearance of blood. John, in his Revelation, had predicted the extraordinary events of that day. After the earthquake, he wrote, the sun would become "black as sackcloth of hair, and the moon . . . like blood" (Rev. 6:12).

Both Jesus and John spoke about a falling of the stars before Christ's return (see Rev. 6:13 and Matt. 24:29). Many Bible scholars believe that this was fulfilled with the great meteoric shower of November 13, 1833. It was the most extensive display of falling stars on record. According to reports, a single observer could see an average of 60,000 meteors per hour. The phenomenon was seen from Canada to Mexico and from the mid-Atlantic to the Pacific. These signs in the heavens heralded the beginning of the time of the end.

An Increase of Knowledge

The prophet Daniel was told, "But you, Daniel, shut up the words, and seal the book until the time of the end; many shall run to and fro, and knowledge shall increase" (Dan. 12:4). As the time of the end began there would be a noticeable increase in knowledge of prophetic things, science, communication, and travel. Without question this prophecy has had a dramatic fulfillment. Just a few examples will have to suffice.

From Horseback to the Moon

The increase of knowledge is very striking. For 59 centuries if someone wanted to travel on land faster or farther than they could walk or run, they rode on the backs of animals or were towed by them. It has been during the past 150 years only that humans have gone from horseback to the moon—literally!

On December 17, 1903, Orville and Wilbur Wright sent a telegram back to their mother, who was minding their bicycle shop in Dayton, Ohio. "Success at last," it read. "We'll be home for Christmas." They had just made the world's first flight in a heavier-than-air machine at Kitty Hawk, North Carolina. Orville piloted the plane, named the *Flyer,* having won the privilege by the toss of a coin. He flew 120 feet and remained in the air for 12 seconds!

The Wrights probably did not foresee how greatly the airplane would change civilization. For example, they did not believe at first that it would ever be possible to fly at night. But these two self-taught engineers, working in a bicycle shop, made the world forever a smaller place. People now travel in jumbo jets, supersonic fighters, space shuttles, and rockets!

Science Springs to Life

1909—Leo Baekeland developed the first all-artificial plastic. Setting out to make an insulator, he invented the first true plastic and transformed the world.

1916—Albert Einstein proposed the general theory of relativity. The scientific touchstones of the modern age—the atomic bomb, space travel, electronics, quantum physics—all bear his imprint.

1923—Edwin Hubble proved that the universe extends far beyond the edges of the Milky Way galaxy. His discovery that the universe is expanding was one of the great intellectual revolutions of the twentieth century.

1926—Robert Goddard launched the first liquid-fueled rocket to an altitude of 41 feet. He launched the space age with that 10-foot rocket from a New England cabbage field.

1927—Philo Farnsworth developed the first electronic scanning system. The key to the television picture tube came to him at age 14, when he was still a farmboy. He had a working device at age 21.

1928—Alexander Fleming identified penicillin. A spore that drifted into his lab and took root on a culture dish started a chain of events that altered forever the treatment of bacterial infections.

1947—William Shockly, along with Bardeen and Brattain, invented the transistor. It replaced vacuum tubes with semiconducting crystals and brought the silicon to Silicon Valley.

1955—Jonas Salk's polio vaccine was proved effective. He became a national hero as "the man who saved the children."

Obviously the list could go on, with a long list of inventors and inventions. We now commonly use microwave ovens, radar, lasers, high-tech photography, computers, the Internet, pagers, cellular phones, satellite global positioning systems, virtual reality systems, and much more. There is no question to any observer that knowledge has literally exploded in the twentieth century.

Wars and Rumors of Wars

There have been wars ever since Cain killed Abel. The conquest of nations down through time has almost always been determined by bloody battles. Jesus told His disciples that there would continue to be wars and rumors of wars, with nation rising against nation and kingdom against kingdom (Matt. 24:6, 7). The significance of this as a sign would be if the wars were much larger and more consequential than those previously fought.

Here, just as in the remarkable increase of knowledge, the war story is told only in superlatives. In the two great world wars in the twentieth century more than 69 million military and civilian personnel were killed. That is more than the combined total of all of earth's other recorded wars! World War II killed more people, cost more money (more than $1 trillion), damaged more property, affected more people, and probably caused more far-reaching changes than any other war in history. It extended to almost every part of the world. The chief battlegrounds included Asia, Europe, North Africa, the Atlantic and Pacific oceans, and the Mediterranean Sea. More than 50 countries took part in the war, and the entire world felt its effects.

But after referring to wars, Jesus added, "the end

is not yet" (verse 6). Other signs would follow in the countdown to the end.

Financial Problems

Many New Testament passages indicate that the economy would be a major factor in the end-time scenario. For example, 2 Timothy 3:1-5 gives a long list of signs that begins with the fact that people would be selfish and covetous. And James 5:1-6 indicates that people would be attempting to get rich and would heap up treasure for the last days. They would live in luxury and pleasure while others around them are struggling just to get by. Yet finally people will realize the futility of earthly treasure and will cast their idols of silver and gold to the moles and the bats (Isa. 2:20).

Advertisements in popular magazines shout, "Others are making millions in the stock market. Jump in and get your share!" The market reports are part of every major news broadcast. But behind the lure of wealth, the financial picture is beginning to lose its silver lining.

Two factors dominate the financial markets—fear and greed. The market had many wild fluctuations during 1998. Primarily because of fear of a worldwide economic meltdown and the overvaluation of many publicly traded stocks, the price of common stock plunged and then rebounded.

A typical fear/greed cycle looks like this: People begin to realize that the world economy is failing fast. They look at the U.S. stock market and realize that many stocks are selling for a price that is more than 100 times the value or net worth of the company they represent. They then begin to sell off stock. With so much stock on the market, the price per share begins to fall. Those holding the stock get worried—read "frightened"—and they want to sell their stock before the market falls even further. Computer-generated "sell" signals begin to sell off falling stock automatically. The snowball effect causes a severe drop in the market. As the selloff slows, greed kicks back in, "bargain hunters" start buying stock, and the cost per share rises—until fear kicks in again to begin yet another cycle.

The stock market is just one indicator that there are serious economic times just ahead. Some of the other factors are listed below.

The dramatic rise in personal bankruptcy. In every year in the 1990s there has been a dramatic increase over the previous year's record of personal bankruptcies in the United States. For example, by the end of the third quarter of 1998 more than 25,000 personal bankruptcies were being filed each week. The unwise use of credit cards is frequently the cause of personal bankruptcy.

The Asian "flu." Typically the Pacific Rim nations have been the major trading partners for the United States. However, they have gotten financially sick. It all started when Thailand devalued its currency in early July 1998. The "flu" quickly spread across Asia. Even Japan, our major partner, has taken a major economic hit. Things got so bad in Japan that in less than a year 15 major bankers and stockbrokers committed suicide; the wives of many of them joined them in death. In late July Japanese prime minister

Hashimoto suddenly resigned his position, accepting blame for having failed to bring Japan out of the worst economic recession since World War II. At the end of the third quarter the 19 top banks in Japan together had only 8 percent loan capitalization. In other words, if only 8 percent of their current loans failed—which is highly likely, given the current economic state—many of the banks would fail.

Russia's great recession. In August 1998 Russia defaulted on $40 billion in short-term debts and devalued the ruble. Eighteen of 20 major Russian banks effectively failed under high debts. The deteriorating financial condition in Russia pushed a giant U.S. hedge fund to the brink of failure. A federal reserve bank rescue effort saved it—and perhaps prevented a global financial meltdown.

Big banks get bashed. At the end of the third quarter of 1998 the big banks really took a hit. Exploding hedge funds, falling currencies, and bad loans added up to a miserable quarter. Bankers Trust had a third-quarter loss of $488 million and expected to have to lay off 10 percent of its staff. BankAmerica's losses were so embarrassingly large that president David Coulter was forced to resign. The bank took $900 million in write-downs and trading losses, with more than a third of that—$372 million—the result of a soured loan to a high-roller hedge fund, D. E. Shaw & Co.

The list goes on—Citigroup had a 53 percent drop in third-quarter profits because of $1 billion in trading losses and write-downs. They were expected to lay off 5 percent of their staff—8,000 jobs. J. P. Morgan Bank had a 61 percent decline in third-quarter profits and a $56 million trading loss. Chase Manhattan wrote off $200 million in bad loans.

The big trading companies have also been showing signs of distress. Merrill Lynch announced layoffs, and in September 1998 Salomon Smith Barney's global trading division announced a $360 million loss. The cover of *Forbes* magazine's September 21, 1998, issue asked in bold letters: "Is it Armageddon?"

The ballooning U.S. trade deficit. The U.S. trade deficit is ballooning, as exports drop and other countries try to recover by selling more to the United States. Many containers that are shipped full of goods to American markets return to Asia empty. The International Monetary Fund projected that the current account deficit for broadly defined trade would hit $290 billion in 1999, almost double the $155 billion in 1997. In a six-month period in 1998 manufacturing jobs fell by 152,000. Since the U.S.'s trading partners are not buying U.S. goods, that leaves it mostly up to the American consumer to keep the sale of goods steady. Unfortunately, Americans are already spending almost all of their current income, and spending way beyond their means in credit card purchases.

A Decline in Moral Values

One of the greatest evidences of the decline of moral values in society today is the extreme tolerance that is expressed toward wrongdoing. The I'm-OK-you're-OK mentality concludes, I'm no worse than you are. Or: Everybody's doing it so it must be OK.

December 27, 1998, just days after the House of

Representatives voted to impeach President Bill Clinton, the Washington *Post* gave front-page attention to the changing moral values of America. The paper stated, "The sharply divided public reaction to the impeachment of President Clinton has provided a dramatic showcase of a struggle for American values that goes back to the 1960s and remains unresolved today.

"As an emblematic figure from that troubled decade, polls and analysts said, Clinton confronts his fellow citizens with choices between deeply held moral standards and an abhorrence of judging others' behavior. . . .

"Few issues are more revealing than Clinton's impeachment when it comes to highlighting how values have changed over the past 30 years. Almost without exception, experts interviewed said the public verdict in his case is far different than it would have been in the late sixties because the values environment has changed."

The Bible predicted this type of society as a sign of the last days. "But know this, that in the last days perilous times will come: for men will be lovers of themselves, lovers of money, boasters, proud, blasphemers, disobedient to parents, unthankful, unholy, unloving, unforgiving, slanderers, without self-control, brutal, dispisers of good, traitors, headstrong, haughty, lovers of pleasure rather than lovers of God, having a form of godliness but denying its power. And from such people turn away!" (2 Tim. 3:1-5).

Without Self-control, Brutal

By the time the typical American teenager turns

18, he or she has seen 40,000 dramatized murders and 200,000 other dramatized acts of violence. Are the young people of today natural-born killers? In the August 10, 1998, isssue of *Christianity Today,* Lt. Col. Dave Grossman argued persuasively that the media are desensitizing youth to violence, conditioning them to associate violence with pleasure and, through simulator-type video games, even giving them the skills to kill with guns. In the May 3, 1999, issue of *U.S. News & World Report,* John Leo quotes Grossman as saying that "Michael Carneal, the schoolboy shooter in Paducah, Kentucky, showed the effects of video-game lessons in killing. Carneal coolly shot nine times, hitting eight people, five of them in the head or neck. Head shots pay a bonus in many video games."

Regarding the Columbine High School massacre Leo asked, "Was it real life or an acted-out video game?

"Marching through a large building using various bombs and guns to pick off victims is a conventional video-game scenario. In the Colorado massacre, Dylan Klebold and Eric Harris used pistol-grip shotguns, as in some video-arcade games. The pools of blood, screams of agony, and pleas for mercy must have been familiar—they are featured in some of the newer and more realistic kill-for-kicks games. 'With each kill,' the Los Angeles *Times* reported, 'the teens cackled and shouted as though playing one of the morbid video games they loved.' And they ended their spree by shooting themselves in the head, the final act in the game Postal, and, in fact, the only way to end it" *(ibid.).*

We are not talking about isolated incidents here. A pattern of violence has developed that can be recognized only as an unusual prevalence—a sign of the end. Barry Loukaitis, 14, of Moses Lake, Washington, killed a teacher and two students and wounded one other on February 2, 1996. Luke Woodham, 16, of Pearl, Mississippi, on October 1, 1997, killed two students, wounded seven, and stabbed his mother to death. Michael Carneal, 14, of West Paducah, Kentucky, on December 1, 1997, killed three students and wounded five others. Andrew Golden, 11, and Mitchell Johnson, 13, of Jonesboro, Arkansas, on March 24, 1998, killed a teacher and four fellow students and wounded 10 others. Kipland Kinkel, 15, of Springfield, Oregon, on May 21, 1998, killed two students and wounded 22 and then killed both of his parents. Eric Harris, 18, and Dylan Klebold, 17, of Littleton, Colorado, on April 20, 1999, killed one teacher and 12 fellow students and wounded 23 others. Thomas Solomon, 15, of Conyers, Georgia, on May 20, 1999, wounded six fellow students.

Illegal drug use has continued to plague society. Now even in rural small-town America drug problems escalate as a menace to law-abiding citizens.

Porn goes public. High technology and high finance are making the smut business look legitimate. How did this happen? *Forbes*, June 14, 1999, reported: "A turning point in the industrialization of pornography came in 1973. That was when the Supreme Court ruled in *Miller v. California* that 'pornography' but not 'obscenity' was protected by the First Amendment.

While the Supreme Court began pornography's legal liberation, the biggest obstacle to the distribution of graphic sexual material remained the mob-controlled Times Square sex shops and theaters. Squalor and embarrassment had the effect of enforcing a taboo.

"Technology took care of that: the VCR, the pay-per-view, and now the Internet. The curious discovered they could watch erotica in the privacy of their own home. Result? Last year 8,948 hard-core videos hit the U.S. retail market, up from 1,275 in 1990. In 1998 Americans rented 686 million 'adult' tapes. This year X-rated videos should generate some $5 billion in sales and rentals, double the revenue of five years ago."

Has this private availability of pornography had any effect upon society? Ask Lutheran minister Ronald Thiemann, former dean of the Harvard Divinity School. *Newsweek,* May 31, 1999, told his story under the heading "An Odd Fall From Grace—Computer Porn Undoes a Divinity-School Dean": "When Ronald Thiemann asked his university tech-support team to upgrade his hard drive last fall, it seemed like a routine request to turbocharge a data-clogged computer. Nor was there anything unusual about his asking to have his old files transferred to the new hard drive. But the operation proved anything but routine. A techie's curious eye caught sight of an extensive collection of hard-core pornography. Less than a month later Thiemann suddenly went on sabbatical 'to spend time with my family.' Last week the Boston *Globe* reported: Thiemann, dean of Harvard's Divinity School, has lost his post over porn."

The worldwide AIDS epidemic continues as a

scourge on civilization. At the end of 1998 the news reported that in Africa alone more than 5,500 people die of AIDS every day! And yet it is politically incorrect to talk about the causes or prevention of AIDS. A society has developed that tolerates widespread divorce, adultery, and casual drug use as if it were "normal" behavior. Where can this lead but to the downfall of our culture?

Natural Disasters

Early in 1998 climatologists began warning of a developing weather pattern called El Niño. It came! California alone was hit with $500 million in damage from pounding rains, mud slides, high winds, and record surfs. Forty-two of the state's 58 counties were declared disaster areas. Record tornadoes in central Florida in February 1998 killed 42 people and did $100 million in damage.

Fires. In June 1998 hundreds of fires ravaged the state of Florida and scorched nearly 500,000 acres. Of Florida's 67 counties, only Monroe County, which is comprised of the waterbound chain of islands called the Florida Keys, escaped the fire. At one point firefighters from 41 states, and more than two thirds of the water-carrying helicopters in the entire country, were on the scene. More than 350 homes and businesses and dozens of vehicles were destroyed or damaged. The fires were not limited to Florida. In fact, fires raged out of control in places all over the world. Four examples will demonstrate their severity. In Central America fire consumed 2,150 *square miles*. In Mexico more than 940,000 acres were charred. In Brazil some 20,000 square miles—an area about half the size of the state of New York—were engulfed. And in Indonesia 7,700 square miles of forest land burned, spreading smoke and haze to such nations as Malaysia and the Philippines, making it tough for 70 million people to breathe easily.

Earthquakes. The rise in global quakes is both astounding and alarming. In the nineteenth century there were only 2,119 recorded earthquakes. In comparison, in the single year of 1993 there were 21,476 recorded. Earthquakes have always been a part of earth's history, but we are now witnessing a phenomenal increase in both frequency and intensity. For example, before the twentieth century there were only 10 major earthquakes recorded. Now we are recording more than 3,000 major earthquakes (over 6 on the Richter scale) each year! In the past 90 years 1.5 million people have been killed in earthquakes.

Floods. Few natural disasters have been as destructive as the floods of 1998. The typical annual rainfall in the sleepy little border town of Del Rio, Texas, is 17 inches. But on Sunday, August 23, 1998, a flash flood caused by Tropical Storm Charley dumped 18 inches on the city in just one day. The nearby Rio Grande and its tributaries spilled over their banks, and by the time the storm subsided 16 people had been killed. Two months after the tragedy 20 people were still missing.

Only superlatives could describe the extent of the worldwide flooding in 1998. I will mention just a few highlights. The flooding in Kenya in January was the worst in the country's history. In Bangladesh floods caused by monsoon rains killed 1,050 people, left 25 million homeless or stranded, and left 80 percent of the country under water and thousands of people facing starvation.

In August torrential rain caused China's Yangtze River to roar through the surrounding area at an estimated rate of 2 million cubic feet of water per second. Throughout the region more than 5.6 million houses were washed away. The disaster caused $30 billion in damage and affected 230 million people— more than 20 percent of the population of the entire country! This enormous flood killed 3,656 people, according to Chinese government statistics. However, Western observers feel that the actual count could be 10 times that number.

Closer to home, during late October and early November of 1998 Hurricane Mitch caused the most flood damage in Honduras, Nicaragua, and Guatemala in decades—maybe ever. *Time* magazine, November 16, 1998, headlined the story: "Murderous Mitch—The Hurricane That Devastated Central America Killed Thousands and Slaughtered the Hopes of Millions."

In Honduras, perhaps the worst-hit country, more than 7,000 died and more than 11,000 were missing and presumed dead. Public schools officially closed for the year; those school buildings that were still usable were turned into emergency shelters for the almost 2 million homeless in a country of 6 million. It has been determined that Hurricane Mitch was the most intensive and destructive natural disaster to occur in the Western Hemisphere. In addition, 1998 has been declared the most significant year in world history for natural disasters.

The twister from hell. On May 3, 1999, one of the world's most powerful and destructive tornadoes hit the state of Oklahoma. At times it was up to a mile wide, and it cut a path of destruction for more than 80 miles. The storm laid waste suburban neighborhoods like a combine mowing wheat. In one disastrous day more than 10,000 homes were destroyed; property damage was estimated at more than $1 billion in Oklahoma alone. The big tornado's top speed was measured by the University of Oklahoma at 318 miles an hour, the highest wind ever recorded on earth! This was an F5 on the Fujita scale, or, as meteorologist Harold Brooks of the National Severe Storms Laboratory puts it, "a moose." But it was only the biggest of 76 tornadoes that hit Texas, Oklahoma, and Kansas on that same day—killing more than 46 people and injuring more than 700. The story is much bigger than this brief report, but do I need to say more?

A Critical Mass

This has been just a quick cross-section of life in our modern world. We haven't mentioned famines, disease, drought, or signs in the religious world. We could discuss the ecumenical movement, the adjoining of church and state in the matter of vouchers for education, the Lutheran/Catholic agreement that apologizes for the Reformation, the pope's letter *Dies Domini* urging worldwide Sunday observance, etc. But the evidence should be clear to all who care to observe that the signs that Jesus and the Bible writers gave as indicators of the end of the world are being fulfilled in detail. The convergence of the Bible's great time prophecies and the signs of the end result in a critical mass of evidence. Surely we are almost home.

Chapter Nine

THE ROAD BACK

for centuries the teachings of the Christian church were a mixture of Scripture and tradition. But in God's providence the time came to give Scripture its rightful place and to make the Bible available to the people. The Protestant Reformation began the long road back to biblical fidelity. Many who were studying the Bible for the first time longed to learn the true biblical faith. Others stuck with tradition, too apathetic to change.

In the fourteenth century John Wycliffe called for a reformation of the church, not just in England but in the entire Christian world. At that time the Bible was not readily available to the common person. Wycliffe provided the first translation of the entire Bible into

English. He is now called the morning star of the Reformation because his teachings of salvation through faith in Christ alone and that the Scriptures alone were to be the source of Christian faith and practice laid the foundation for the great Protestant Reformation. His teachings had a major influence on other Reformers such as Huss, Jerome, and Luther.

God used Martin Luther in Germany to further this change. As a young priest, Luther was disturbed by the sale of indulgences by the church. This was the payment of money to the church in exchange for forgiveness of personal sins as well as the sins of those who were suffering in the flames of purgatory. To Luther, this was bad theology. He wrote out 95 reasons he felt this was unbiblical, and nailed them to the church door in Wittenberg. This action put Luther in direct confrontation with papal authority and was the primary spark that ignited the Reformation. In spite of the almost overwhelming power of the Papacy to frighten those in opposition to her teachings, Luther stood firm in his two great convictions— that salvation was by faith in Christ alone and that the Scriptures are the only standard for Christian faith and practice.

The Long Road Back

Let me use a few illustrations to describe the problem encountered by the Reformation. First, the church didn't get in its fallen condition overnight. It was a gradual fall over literally centuries of time. It couldn't be changed overnight, either. This is much like a person who after years of inactivity and overeating decides to get on a fitness program. To tone up and lose weight can't be done overnight. The lifestyle must be changed and health reclaimed.

Because the apostasy transpired over many centuries it was almost imperceptible to any individual at any point in time. It's somewhat like the growing-up process of a child. The child may not notice much change. But when he or she makes a visit to Grandma's after a year's lapse, Grandma exclaims, "Oh, how much you have grown!" Similarly, a person may not notice much, if any, change in the church; that is because it is too gradual. But over time the church has gone so far from the path to the kingdom that very few even remember what that path looks like.

Another factor is the level of mental sharpness of the church. The Bible describes the church at the end as being asleep (Matt. 25:5). Quite often those who are asleep do not enjoy being awakened. But the Bible gives us many warnings to wake up. "And do this, knowing the time, that now it is high time to awake out of sleep; for now our salvation is nearer than when we first believed. The night is far spent, the day is at hand. Therefore let us cast off the works of darkness, and let us put on the armor of light. Let us walk properly, as in the day, not in revelry and drunkenness, not in lewdness and lust, not in strife and envy. But put on the Lord Jesus Christ, and make no provision for the flesh, to fulfill its lusts" (Rom. 13:11-14).

During the early period of the Reformation many of the unbiblical teachings of the church, such as prayers for the dead, veneration of saints and relics, celebration of the Mass, worship of Mary, purgatory, penance, holy water, celibacy of the priesthood, the rosary, the Inquisition, transubstantiation, extreme unction, and dependence upon tradition, were repudiated and abandoned. In fact, the Protestant Reformers were nearly unanimous in identifying the papal system as the "man of sin," the "mystery of iniquity," and the "little horn" of Daniel 7. They saw it as the entity that was to persecute God's true people during the 1,260 years of Revelation 12:6, 14 and 13:5, before the second coming of Jesus.

Why So Many Denominations?

The reformation of the Christian church should not have ended in the sixteenth century. The Reformers made much progress, but they did not rediscover all the light lost during the apostasy. They took Christianity out of deep darkness, but it still stood in the shadows. They broke the vicelike grip of the medieval church, gave the Bible to the people in their own languages, and restored the basic gospel. But there were many other Bible truths, such as baptism by immersion, immortality as a gift given by Christ at the time of the resurrection of the righteous, the seventh day as the Bible Sabbath, and other basic Bible truths waiting to be rediscovered.

The successors of the early Reformers failed to advance in Bible knowledge much beyond their predecessors. In fact, many called themselves by the names of the Reformers and did not study further to seek even more of the forgotten truths. This led to the many different denominations in the Protestant world. People who followed each Reformer camped around these great individuals but for some reason would not accept any further light than their leader had discovered. It was apparently God's idea, however, for each generation to stand on the foundation laid by former students of the Bible and build on that until the entire truth of God's Word would be restored.

The Devil and the Church

The twelfth chapter of the book of Revelation gives a brief but explicit history of the New Testament church and reveals the characteristics of the last or remnant of that church. A great red dragon is pictured as about to pounce on the woman clothed with the sun. Already it had brought about the downfall of one third of heaven's angels (Rev. 12:4, 7-10). Now if it could devour the Infant about to be born to the woman, it would win the war.

The woman standing before the dragon is clothed with the sun and has the moon under her feet; she wears a crown of 12 stars. The male Child, to whom she gives birth is destined to "rule all nations with a rod of iron." The dragon attacks the Child but its efforts to kill the Child are not successful. Instead, the Child is "caught up to God and His throne" (verse 5).

The angry dragon then turns his attention to the woman, the Child's mother, who is miraculously given wings and is taken into the wilderness to a place prepared for her by God. There God feeds and takes care of her for a time and times and half a time—three and a half prophetic years, or 1,260 prophetic days (Rev. 12:13, 14). This is obviously the same prophetic time period during which the true church suffered persecution at the hands of the little-horn power of Daniel 7. Now, let's see if we can figure out all this symbolic language.

In Bible prophecy a pure woman represents God's faithful church. A woman described as a fornicator or adulterer represents God's people who have apostatized (Eze. 16; Isa. 57:8; Jer. 31:4, 5; Hosea 1-3; Rev. 17:1-5). The dragon is the "serpent of old, called the Devil and Satan" (Rev. 12:9), who was waiting to devour the male Child—the long-expected Messiah, Jesus Christ. The dragon used as his instruments of death the Roman Empire and the apostatized people of God. But nothing, not even death on the cross, could distract Jesus from His mission as the Saviour of humankind.

Christ defeated Satan by dying on the cross. Speaking of His crucifixion, Jesus said, "Now is the judgment of this world; now the ruler of this world will be cast out" (John 12:31). With this great event the heavenly choir sings the song of victory with a loud voice. "Now salvation, and strength, and the kingdom of our God, and the power of His Christ have come, for the accuser of our brethren, who accused them before our God day and night, has been cast down. . . . Therefore rejoice, O heavens, and you who dwell in them!" (Rev. 12:10-12).

But while heaven rejoices, earth must take warning: "Woe to the inhabitants of the earth and the sea! For the devil has come down to you, having great wrath, because he knows that he has a short time" (verse 12). As we have discovered in this book, the great prophetic clock is running out of time.

Apparently the devil's intensity at the end is fueled by the fact that he knows that time is short. God's people are almost home!

As we have noted, true to the prophecy the church was persecuted for 1,260 prophetic days or 1,260 literal years. But though the church suffered greatly, it still survived. Though God's faithful people were scattered all over the earth—"the wilderness"—God provided protection for them. At the end of this prophetic period, which, as we have seen earlier, ended in 1798, God's true people began to emerge and join together in response to the signs of Christ's soon return. John describes this faithful group as "the rest of her offspring . . . who keep the commandments of God, and have the testimony of Jesus Christ" (verse 17). This same verse indicates that the devil hates this remnant group and makes war with it.

Looking for the Remnant

Naturally, those who are looking for biblical truth and are making preparation for meeting Jesus at His second coming will be interested in becoming a part of His last-day church. The church is important to Jesus. He organized it, gave His life for it, and gave gifts to it. But how does one find the true church today? The book of Revelation gives two almost identical descriptions of this group. The first is where we have just been studying—Revelation 12:17. This verse contains a description of the last remnant in God's chosen line of loyal believers—His loyal witnesses in the last days just before Christ's second coming. "And the dragon was enraged with the woman, and he went to make war with the rest of her offspring, who keep the commandments of God and have the testimony of Jesus Christ." Here, in this description of the devil's battle with the last-day church, John used the expression "the rest of her offspring." That expression means the "remaining ones" or "remnant" (KJV).

The other description given by John of the last-day faithful ones is in Revelation 14:12. It states, "Here is the patience of the saints; here are those who keep the commandments of God and the faith of Jesus." So the remnant at the time of the end cannot easily be mistaken. The Bible describes them in specific terms. They keep the commandments of God and have the testimony of Jesus Christ. In addition, they have the responsibility of proclaiming, just before Jesus returns, God's final message of warning to the world. That message is recorded in Revelation 14:6-12. Let us consider more closely each of these characteristics.

The characteristic is "the faith of Jesus." God's remnant people are characterized by a faith similar to that which Jesus had. They reflect Jesus' unshakable confidence in God and the authority of Scripture. They believe that Jesus Christ is the Messiah of prophecy, the Son of God, who came as the Saviour of the world. Their faith encompasses all the truths of the Bible— those that Jesus and the apostles believed and taught.

Accordingly, God's remnant people will proclaim the everlasting gospel of salvation by faith in Christ. They will warn the world that the hour of God's judgment has arrived. (We will cover the aspect of the great pre-Advent judgment of God in the next chapter.) Like Elijah and John the Baptist, the remnant will prepare the way of the Lord. They will proclaim the soon-coming Lord. They will be involved in a great worldwide mission to complete the divine witness to humanity (Rev. 14:6, 7; 10:11; Matt. 24:14).

The second characteristic of the remnant is that they "keep the commandments of God." In any generation those who return to the Lord will keep His commandments. Genuine faith in Jesus commits the remnant to follow His example. "He who says he abides in Him," John said, "ought himself also to walk just as He walked" (1 John 2:6). Jesus kept His Father's commandments, and they too will obey God's commandments (John 15:10).

Inasmuch as they are the remnant, God's last-day church will practice what the early church preached. And their actions must harmonize with their profession. Jesus said, "Not everyone who says to Me, 'Lord, Lord,' shall enter the kingdom of heaven, but he who does the will of My Father in heaven" (Matt. 7:21). Through the strength Christ gives them, they obey God's requirements, including all 10 of the commandments, God's unchanging moral law (Ex. 20:1-17; Matt. 5:17-19; 19:17; Phil. 4:13). Obviously this will include the restoration of the keeping of the seventh-day Sabbath, the fourth commandment.

This was predicted of the remnant by the prophet Isaiah. "Those from among you shall build the old waste places; you shall raise up the foundations of many generations; and you shall be called the Repairer of the Breach, the Restorer of Streets to

Dwell In. If you turn away your foot from the Sabbath, from doing your pleasure on My holy day, and call the Sabbath a delight, the holy day of the Lord honorable, and shall honor Him, not doing your own ways, nor finding your own pleasure, nor speaking your own words, then you shall delight yourself in the Lord; and I will cause you to ride on the high hills of the earth, and feed you with the heritage of Jacob your father. The mouth of the Lord has spoken" (Isa. 58:12-14).

Right on time, just when the end-time prophecies began their fulfillment, Christians rediscovered the seventh-day Sabbath and began to keep it holy. Christian Sabbathkeepers now number in the millions, and thousands more are joining them every day. The Seventh-day Adventist Church has been at the forefront in this movement.

A third characteristic of God's remnant people at the end of time is that they possess "the testimony of Jesus." John defines "the testimony of Jesus" as "the spirit [or gift] of prophecy" (Rev. 19:10). The remnant will be guided by the testimony of Jesus conveyed through the gift of prophecy. This gift of the Spirit was to function continuously throughout the history of the church, until "all come to the unity of the faith and the knowledge of the Son of God, to a perfect man, to the measure of the stature of the fullness of Christ" (Eph. 4:13). It is therefore one of the major characteristics of the remnant.

The Bible says that when Jesus returned to heaven after His first advent He "gave gifts to men" (verse 8). In five places the New Testament names some of these divine gifts to the Christian church: Romans 12:6-8; 1 Corinthians 12:4-11; 1 Corinthians 13:1-3; 1 Corinthians 14; and Ephesians 4:11-16. It is significant to note that only one gift occurs in all five places. It is the gift of prophecy! Apparently our Lord Jesus recognized the need for continuing contact with His people, especially as the time of the end approached. It would not be like God, who has communicated with humans down through the ages, to abandon them at the very end, right before the most climactic event since the Creation. We know that "the Lord God does nothing, unless He reveals His secret to His servants the prophets" (Amos 3:7).

Such prophetic guidance makes the remnant a people of prophecy who proclaim a prophetic message. They will understand prophecy and teach it and have the gift of prophecy in their midst. The revelation of truth that comes to the remnant helps them accomplish their mission of preparing the world for Christ's return.

The timing of the work of the remnant is another characteristic of this group. The Bible indicates that the remnant appears on the world's stage after the time of the great persecution (Rev. 12:14-17). The earthshaking events of the French Revolution, which led to the captivity of the pope at the end of the 1,260-year period in 1798 and the fulfillment of the three great cosmic signs—in which the sun, moon, and stars testified of the nearness of Christ's return (see the previous chapter)—led to a major revival of the study of prophecy. Many were convinced that the second coming of Christ was imminent. Throughout the world many Christians recognized that "the time of the end" had arrived (Dan. 12:4).

As Christians saw the fulfillment of many Bible prophecies during the second half of the eighteenth and the first half of the nineteenth century, a powerful interconfessional revival movement took place that centered on the Second Advent hope. This hope brought a deep spirit of unity among its adherents, and many joined together to proclaim to the world Christ's soon return. This movement was centered on the Word of God. People were convinced that God was calling a remnant to continue the reformation of the Christian church.

The Remnant People Give the Last Warning to the World

The book of Revelation clearly outlines the message and mission of the remnant people of God. Their message is so important that it is represented as angel messengers flying in midheaven and crying with loud voices. The Bible records the messages in Revelation 14:6-12. The timing is so precise that they could only be from heaven. These three messages comprise God's answers to the overwhelming satanic deception that sweeps the world just before Christ returns (Rev. 13:3, 8, 14-16). Then immediately after the giving of God's last appeal to the world, Christ returns to reap the harvest of the earth (Rev. 14:14-20). As we travel the road back toward the kingdom of God we must all respond to these messages and in turn share them with the world.

The First Angel's Message

"Then I saw another angel flying in the midst of heaven, having the everlasting gospel to preach to those who dwell on the earth—to every nation, tribe, tongue, and people—saying with a loud voice, 'Fear God and give glory to Him, for the hour of His judgment has come; and worship Him who made heaven and earth, the sea and springs of water'" (Rev. 14:6, 7).

This first message given by the remnant contains the everlasting gospel. In view of the judgment they reaffirm the everlasting gospel that sinners can be justified by faith and receive Christ's righteousness. The message—virtually the same as given by Elijah and John the Baptist—calls the world to repentance. It calls for everyone to "fear" or reverence God, and to give "glory" or honor to Him.

This call to the world also announces that "the hour of His judgment has come." This adds urgency to the message. I will cover this aspect of the message in some detail in the next chapter.

Next comes the call to worship the Creator. By commanding us to "worship Him who made heaven and earth, the sea and springs of water" this message calls attention back to the fourth commandment. This is easy to conclude when we compare this passage (Rev. 14:7) with the fourth commandment (Ex. 20: 8-11). This first message leads people into true worship of the Creator, an experience that involves honoring His memorial of Creation—the seventh-day Sabbath of the Lord. God instituted the Sabbath at Creation (Gen. 2:1-3) and affirmed it in the Ten Commandments (Ex. 20:8-11). In addition to the Sabbath being a memorial of Creation, it is also a sign that God is the One who sanctifies the keeper. "Surely My Sabbaths you shall keep, for it is a sign between Me and you throughout your generations, that you may know that I am the Lord who sanctifies you" (Ex. 31:13; see also Eze. 20:12). Unfortunately this important sign of God's Creation and redemption is neglected by the vast majority of God's created beings.

The Second Angel's Message

"Babylon is fallen, is fallen, that great city, because she has made all nations drink of the wine of the wrath of her fornication" (Rev. 14:8).

From early history the city of Babylon symbolized defiance of God. Its tower was a monument to apostasy and a center of rebellion. Throughout the Bible the struggle between God's city, Jerusalem, and Satan's city, Babylon, illustrates the conflict between good and evil. Because of the apostasy and persecution, most Protestants of the Reformation and post-Reformation era have referred to the church of Rome as spiritual Babylon, the enemy of God's people. Revelation 17 gives a study of the false religious system just as Revelation 12 describes the true church.

The message of the second angel brings out the universal nature of the Babylonian apostasy and her coercive power, saying that "she has made all nations drink of the wine of the wrath of her fornication." The "wine" of Babylon represents her heretical teachings. Apparently Babylon will pressure the powers of state to enforce universally her false religious teachings and decrees. The "fornication" that is mentioned here represents the illicit relationship between Babylon and the nations, that is, between the apostate church and civil powers. The church is supposed to be married to Christ and to get her support from Him. Accordingly, when she seeks the support of the state she commits spiritual fornication (see James 4:4).

Babylon is said to have fallen because she rejects the message of the first angel—the gospel of righteousness by faith in the Creator. Just as the church of Rome apostatized during the first few centuries of the Christian era, so many Protestants have departed from the great Bible truths of the Reformation or never went beyond their leaders in seeking truth. Sadly, this fall of Babylon involves much of the Christian world. And so the angel depicted in Revelation 18 says, "Come out of her, my people, lest you share in her sins, and lest you receive of her plagues" (verse 4).

The Third Angel's Message

" 'If anyone worships the beast and his image, and receives his mark on his forehead or on his hand, he himself shall also drink of the wine of the wrath of God, which is poured out full strength into the cup of His indignation. He shall be tormented with fire and brimstone in the presence of the holy angels and in the presence of the Lamb. And the smoke of their torment ascends forever and ever; and they have no rest day or night, who worship the beast and his image, and whoever receives the mark of his name.' Here is the patience of the saints; here are those who keep the commandments of God and the faith of Jesus" (Rev. 14:9-12).

The message of the third angel proclaims God's most solemn warning against worshiping the beast and his image. Everyone who rejects these messages from God will ultimately worship the beast. As we have discussed earlier, the beast described in Revelation 13:1-10 is the church-state union that dominated the Christian world during the 1,260-year period. This apostate church was described by Paul as the "man of sin" (2 Thess. 2:3, 4) and by the prophet Daniel as the "little horn" (Dan. 7:8, 20-25; 8:9-12). Accordingly, the image of the beast represents that form of apostate religion that will be developed when churches that have lost the true spirit of the Reformation will unite with the state to enforce their teachings on others. This union of church and state will be a perfect image to the beast.

We are informed by this message that during the final conflict between good and evil two distinct classes will be found. One class will advocate a gospel of tradition and human devisings and will worship the beast and his image. They will bring upon themselves the most grievous judgments. The other class, by contrast, will live by the true gospel and "keep the commandments of God and the faith of Jesus" (Rev. 14:12). The bottom-line final issue will involve true and false worship—the true and the false gospel. When this issue is clearly brought before the world, those who reject God's memorial of His creatorship— the Bible Sabbath—choosing to worship and honor Sunday in the full knowledge that it is not God's appointed day of worship, will receive the "mark of the beast." This mark is a mark of rebellion. It involves choosing a day that humanity has established in place of the one that God established at Creation and memorialized in the Ten Commandments.

The choice to be involved in either of these two groups involves suffering. So the choice is not an easy one. Those who choose to obey God will experience the wrath of the dragon (Rev. 12:17) and eventually be threatened with death (Rev. 13:15), while those who choose to worship the beast and his image will incur the seven last plagues and finally "the lake of fire" (Rev. 15; 16; 20:14, 15).

But though both choices involve suffering, their results are very different. The worshipers of the Creator will escape the deadly wrath of the dragon and finally stand together with the Lamb on Mount Zion (Rev. 14:1). The worshipers of the beast and his image, on the other hand, receive the full wrath of God and die in the presence of the holy angels and the Lamb (verses 9, 10; Rev. 20:14). God has children in all churches and among the unchurched whom He is calling at this final time for decision. The two ways have never been more significant than now. God is calling people out of apostasy and preparing them for Christ's return.

A Powerful Fourth Angel

God is so compassionate and eager to save those who are presently involved in a false or apostate religious system that He sends a final appeal to the world with such power that the entire world is lit up. John speaks of this final appeal in Revelation 18:

"After these things I saw another angel coming down from heaven, having great authority, and the earth was illuminated with his glory. And he cried mightily with a loud voice, saying, 'Babylon the great is fallen, is fallen, and has become a dwelling place of demons, a prison for every foul spirit, and a cage for every unclean and hated bird! For all the nations have drunk of the wine of the wrath of her fornication, the kings of the earth have committed fornication with her, and the merchants of the earth have become rich through the abundance of her luxury.' And I heard another voice from heaven saying, 'Come out of her, my people, lest you share in her sins, and lest you receive of her plagues. For her sins have reached to heaven, and God has remembered her iniquities'" (verses 1-5).

That voice from heaven is calling to all of us today. It is time for us to take stock of our lives and the direction we are going. If we, for whatever reason, have taken the broad road that most of the rest of the world is traveling—the road that leads to destruction—it's time to take the road back to the Creator God and His commandments. Don't put off this important decision. Your eternal life is at stake. We are almost home!

CHAPTER TEN

ALMOST HOME

The understanding that humankind is nearing the end of the journey to its eternal destiny is beginning to come into focus as we have discussed the great Bible prophecies and the signs of the end that were foretold by Jesus and the Bible writers. One more amazing prophecy will pinpoint our day as the time of the pre-Advent judgment of humanity. It points out clearly the last prophetic date before the second coming of Christ.

One thing is certain from the biblical perspective: We must all face the judgment bar of God. "For God will bring every work into judgment, including every secret thing, whether good or whether evil" (Eccl. 12:14). "For we shall all stand before the judgment seat of Christ" (Rom. 14:10). In that urgent message from heaven, depicted in Revelation as given by angels, we are told that just before the second coming of Christ the warning goes to every nation, tribe, tongue, and people: "Fear God and give glory to Him, for the hour of His judgment has come; and worship Him who made heaven and earth, the sea and springs of water" (Rev. 14:7).

Some Christians have apparently felt that the judgment takes place after the Second Coming, but the Scriptures indicate that the division between the saved and the lost is made before Jesus appears, because He will bring His reward with Him. " 'He who is unjust, let him be unjust still; he who is filthy, let him be filthy still; he who is righteous, let him be righteous still; he who is holy, let him be holy still.' 'And behold, I am coming quickly, and My reward is with Me, to give every one according to his work' " (Rev. 22:11, 12).

In addition, it is clear from Scripture that the wicked are slain at the coming of Christ (2 Thess. 2:8; Luke 17:26-30) and the righteous are taken to heaven to be with Him (John 14:3; 1 Thess. 4:16, 17). Neither of these rewards would be just and fair unless the judgment had already taken place.

It is not like God to be involved in some major aspect of salvation history without revealing that fact to the prophets. "Surely the Lord God does nothing, unless He reveals His secret to His servants the prophets" (Amos 3:7). Not only does the Bible pinpoint the beginning of the pre-Advent judgment, as we will see in this chapter, but it also predicted the timing of the first advent of Christ. So Paul was able to say, "But when the fulness of the time had come, God sent forth His Son, born of a woman, born under the law" (Gal. 4:4).

In the Bible's longest time prophecy, and one of its most amazing, both the timing for the first advent of Christ and that of the pre-Advent judgment are given. In the eighth chapter of Daniel, the faithful prophet-statesman has another vision. Just as the vision of beasts in chapter 7 adds details to Nebuchadnezzar's dream of the metal image, this vision in chapter 8 gives more specific details regarding those nations that would significantly impact the people of God.

In Daniel 8 two more beasts, again representing kingdoms, are shown to him. The first is a ram with two horns. The second horn to come up became higher or bigger than the first horn. We are told plainly in verse 20 that "the ram which you saw, having the two horns—they are the kings [or kingdoms] of Media and Persia."

The second beast looked like a male goat except that it had only one great large horn. Later, when the goat grew very great, the horn was broken and four other horns came up in its place. Finally, out of one of the four horns a little horn came up and grew exceedingly great. Again, the specific interpretation of this beast is given: "And the male goat is the kingdom of Greece. The large horn that is between its eyes is the first king. As for the broken horn and the four that stood up in its place, four kingdoms shall arise out of that nation, but not with its power" (verses 21, 22).

Alexander the Great would surely qualify as the "great horn" of Greece. His empire was not defeated by outsiders while he was in power. However, when he died an untimely death his four generals, Cassander, Lysimachus, Ptolemy, and Seleucus, divided the empire after quarreling among themselves. The little horn in Daniel 8:23-25 is described in much the same language as is used in Daniel 7 to describe the little horn there. Here, apparently, both pagan and papal Rome are depicted by the little horn.

The beasts of Daniel 8 are explained and identified right in the chapter—a great help to students of Bible prophecy. But as to the timing of the future events and the time of the end (verses 13-19), Daniel did not understand. He so states in the last verse of the chapter: "And I, Daniel, fainted and was sick for days; afterward I arose and went about the king's business. I was astonished at the vision, but no one understood it" (verse 27).

Apparently the part Daniel didn't understand was the question that was asked, "How long will the vision be?" (verse 13) and the answer, "And he said to me, 'For two thousand three hundred days; then the sanctuary shall be cleansed'" (verse 14).

In chapter 9, verses 3 through 19, there is recorded Daniel's prayer for wisdom and understanding regarding the vision. He fasted during his time of prayer, confessed his sins and those of his people, appealed to God's mercy, and claimed God's promises. We can learn from Daniel's example in prayer. We can claim God's promises as he did. "Then you will call upon Me and go and pray to Me, and I will listen to you. And you will seek Me and find Me, when you search for Me with all your heart" (Jer. 29:12, 13). God also promised, "It shall come to pass that before they call, I will answer; and while they are still speaking, I will hear" (Isa. 65:24).

True to His word, while Daniel was still praying God sent Gabriel with this message: "I have now come forth to give you skill to understand. At the beginning of your supplications the command went out, and I have come to tell you, for you are greatly beloved; therefore consider the matter, and understand the vision" (Dan. 9:22, 23).

As far as the divine record states, Daniel had received no new vision since the one in Daniel 8, so that must be the one he is concerned about in Daniel 9. In addition, when Gabriel appeared Daniel recognized that he was the same person "whom I had seen in the vision at the beginning" (verse 21). So Gabriel must have been commissioned to make this man "understand the vision" of chapter 8. He had already explained everything except verse 14, which had reference to the cleansing of the sanctuary and to the 2,300 evenings and mornings. As a Jew, Daniel understood the cleansing of the sanctuary illustration and its connection with the judgment. But he was still concerned about the calculation of time. So Gabriel began his explanation with a statement about time.

"Seventy weeks are determined," Gabriel said (verse 24). The Hebrew word here translated "determined" is *chathak*. It is used only this once in the entire Bible. But its meaning is familiar to scholars from its usage outside the Bible. The well-known

Hebrew-English dictionary by Gesenius says that properly it means to "cut" or to "divide." Some ancient rabbis used *chathak* as meaning to "amputate." Since Gabriel had come to explain the 2,300 days, he began by announcing that 490 years were to be "cut" or "amputated" from the longer 2,300 "years." (We apply the same day-year prophetic principle here that we did in Daniel 7, as discussed earlier in this book.)

Commentators are virtually unanimous in saying that Gabriel meant 490 years when he spoke of 70 weeks (of years). Obviously 490 years cannot be "cut" away from 2,300 literal days, which add up to less than seven years, so the solution is quite clear: As in other time prophecies, such as the 42 months of Daniel 7, each day represents a year. Accordingly, the 2,300 days are symbolic and stand for 2,300 actual years.

But when does the 2,300-year period begin? In answering that question in Daniel 9:25, Gabriel divides up the 490 years. These divisions, along with his opening statement, help us to positively identify the time points of this prophecy. The segments of the 490 years are as follows: seven weeks (49 years), 62 weeks (434 years), and one week (seven years). The final week is further divided into halves (3½ years each).

Gabriel's explanation of the starting point of the prophecy begins: "Know therefore and understand, that from the going forth of the command to restore and build Jerusalem . . ." (verse 25). Daniel must have been thrilled with the prospect that a command would be given to restore and build Jerusalem, which now lay in ruins back in his homeland. Does the Bible record any such decree? Yes! Actually there are three of them, all recorded in the book of Ezra. Let's quickly review them.

1. The first decree was issued in about 538 B.C. by Cyrus the Great. It permitted a resettlement of the Jewish exiles in their homeland and authorized them to rebuild for God "a house at Jerusalem." The Jews were allowed to take back the sacred utensils that Nebuchadnezzar had taken from the Temple (see Ezra 1:2-11).

2. The second decree was issued by Darius I Hystaspes around 519 B.C. He basically reaffirmed the decree made by Cyrus allowing the rebuilding of the Temple (see Ezra 6:1-12).

3. The third decree was issued by Artaxerxes I. This decree was apparently the one that Gabriel was referring to, as it was far superior to the first two. It authorized Ezra to appoint magistrates and judges with full political and religious authority to try cases under both Jewish and Persian law, and even to impose the death penalty (see Ezra 7:11-26). This decree finally gave Jerusalem its rebirth—its restoration as a capital city. Gabriel had spoken of the "decree" (singular) to "restore and build Jerusalem." Ezra in effect lumps all the decrees together as though they were one: "according to the command of Cyrus, Darius, and Artaxerxes king of Persia" (Ezra 6:14).

Ezra 7 dates this third and most complete decree: the fifth month of the seventh year of Artaxerxes (verse 8), which fell in the late summer or early autumn of 457 B.C. So we now have the date that begins the 70-week (490-year) prophecy and, of course, it is the same date that begins the 2,300-year prophecy off of which the 490 years were "determined" or cut. It is now simply a matter of calculating the dates of the prophecy. Remember that all this prophetic detail will help us who are living today to realize that we are very near the end of time. Let's quickly run the numbers.

Seven weeks (49 years) from 457 B.C. extends to 408 B.C., when the wall of Jerusalem was finished.

Seventy weeks (490 years)—the entire portion "cut off" of the 2,300 years for God's people (Israel)—from the autumn of 457 B.C. extends to A.D. 34, the time of the stoning of Stephen and the beginning of the gospel going to the Gentiles (A.D. 34 [rather than A.D. 33] is correct, as there is no year 0).

If we subtract the last year—the seventieth week—from the end of the 490 years in A.D. 34 we get A.D. 27, the year that Jesus was baptized and anointed by the Holy Spirit. Then in the middle of that week of seven years, from A.D. 27 to A.D. 34, which would be the spring of A.D. 31, the Messiah would be cut off and cause the sacrifices to cease. The death of Jesus in A.D. 31 fulfilled that prophecy precisely.

We are now ready to find the ending date of the 2,300 years. It is now only a matter of simple math. If we subtract the 490 years that was cut off for the people of God from the 2,300 years we have a balance of 1,810 years. We know that the 490 years ended in A.D. 34. If we add the 1,810 years left on the prophecy to A.D. 34 we come all the way down to the fall of 1844. We can now begin to understand the significance of Daniel 8:14. At the end of the 2,300 days the sanctuary would be "cleansed."

As a Jew, Daniel knew that this was symbolic of what took place in the fall of every year in the Temple services: the cleansing of the sanctuary on the Day of Atonement, the day of judgment. And so the date of 1844 is the last time date given in prophecy. It is the beginning of the pre-Advent judgment. It is a major sign that we are almost home.

Since the special days of the Temple services prefigured the work that Christ would do on behalf of humanity, we can understand the significance of the cleansing of the sanctuary in 1844. For example, the Passover prefigured the work of Christ, the Lamb of God, who died on the Passover day. Similarly, the annual Day of Atonement pointed forward to the time when Christ would begin the cleansing work in the great heavenly sanctuary, the work of judgment.

This simple prophecy, given so long ago—almost 500 years before Christ's first advent—takes the Bible student down to the beginning of the pre-Second Advent judgment. We can now say with confidence the words of Revelation 14:7, "Fear God and give glory to Him, for the hour of His judgment has come." The judgment of human beings is taking place in heaven right now, having begun in 1844.

As I mentioned earlier, there are two major indicators that tell us that we are nearing the end of earthly history. The second coming of Christ cannot be far away. The first indicator is Bible prophecy. In the past few chapters we have reviewed the prophecies of Daniel 2, with its great metal image that God used to outline the course of history from that time to the second coming of Christ. In Daniel 7 we saw the same time span covered, using animals instead of metals. In that chapter new details were added, including the reign of the little-horn power, which took us down to 1798, the beginning of the time of the end.

Revelation 13 reviewed the material of Daniel 7 and then added the United States as a major player in the end-time—when the U.S. had risen to a position of world superpower. We discovered that the time portion of Daniel 8 was explained by the angel Gabriel in Daniel 9. This very significant time prophecy foretold the time of Christ's first advent and revealed the date for the beginning of the pre-Second Advent judgment.

What is the significance of all this? We can now see that those events foretold in prophecy have all come to pass—in precise detail. The nations of Babylon, Medo-Persia, Greece, and Rome have all come and gone in the exact order predicted in the Bible. The Roman Empire was divided into the nations of Europe. The Church of Rome had its period of dominance for 1,260 years, from 538 to 1798. The United States has risen to a place of unrivaled leadership in the world. The Papacy has recovered from its wound of 1798, and the United States entered into full diplomatic relations with the Vatican in 1984. Now we can add to this prophetic journey down through time the Bible's longest time prophecy, which takes us down to 1844 and the beginning of the judgment of humanity. Just like clockwork the prophecies have counted down through time to its end-time events.

We have observed that the second major indicator that we are near the end is the "signs" that the Bible gives to herald the time of the end. These "signs" are actual observable conditions or events that are so significant that when we see them we can know that Jesus is at the very doors. We spent considerable time discussing these signs and their amazing and dramatic fulfillment in the current world situation. Unfortunately, the majority of those living on the earth are completely oblivious to the significance of the signs of the end and the nearness of the second coming of Christ. To them this event will come as a thief in the night. But to those who are waiting, watching, and working it will not be like a thief. This relatively small group will be ready for His appearing.

Paul stated, "But you, brethren, are not in darkness, so that this Day should overtake you as a thief. You are all sons of light and sons of the day. We are not of the night nor of darkness. Therefore let us not sleep, as others do, but let us watch and be sober" (1 Thess. 5:4-6). He admonished the Romans, "And do this, knowing the time, that now it is high time to awake out of sleep; for now our salvation is nearer than when we first believed. The night is far spent, the day is at hand. Therefore let us cast off the works of darkness, and let us put on the armor of light. Let us walk properly, as in the day, not in revelry and drunkenness, not in lewdness and lust, not in strife and envy. But put on the Lord Jesus Christ, and make no provision for the flesh, to fulfill its lusts" (Rom. 13:11-14).

It won't be long now. Ready or not, we are almost home.

CHAPTER ELEVEN

IT'S TIME TO DECIDE

It is estimated that the average person makes about 1,000 choices each day. Only about 200 of those choices are made consciously, and very few in a lifetime are momentous. Many of our decisions, however, lead us either closer to, or farther away from, our ultimate life goal: eternal life with God. Some choices or decisions we make have very serious consequences in this life and may also effect our eternal destiny.

Some decisions ought to be made ahead of time so that the response will be automatic. Let me illustrate. Last year in an area within a 15-mile radius of my home more than 700 deer were killed on the highways. Most were killed at night. It seems they are blinded or confused by the headlights and wait until the last moment to jump out in front of a vehicle.

We see several deer in our yard almost every day. They are always a joy to see in nature, but on the highways they have become more than a nuisance. Our children did a lot of their early driving in this area, so they needed to be aware of the possibility of a deer darting out in front of their car. Since an accident involving a deer and a car is almost always fatal to the deer and frequently does considerable damage to the car and sometimes to the occupants of the car, I encouraged my children to decide ahead of time what they would do if a deer jumped in front of them.

If one has not planned ahead for this type of encounter, the natural, almost subconscious, reaction is to jerk the steering wheel to the right or left to avoid hitting the deer. Unfortunately, this response frequently has dire consequences, such as running into another car if you turn left or running off the road if you turn right. In early 1999 two young women, both college students at the University of Maryland, were traveling on the Baltimore-Washington Parkway when a deer darted out in front of their car. The driver turned abruptly to the right, probably almost without thinking; the car ran off the road and hit a tree. Both girls were killed. If the driver had only decided ahead of time to hold the wheel straight under those circumstances!

So my children and I went over this scenario several times to imprint it into our brains: "If a deer jumps in front of your car, hold the steering wheel straight—do not turn sharply to the right or left. Slow down if you have time, but do not turn." The reasoning behind this counsel is quite straightforward. A deer has fast reflexes and can jump quickly. If you hold straight it will have a better chance of avoiding a collision. If you turn, you might hit the deer anyway, but you could also hit another car, a person, or a fixed object.

It is decision time! Men, women, and young people—all of us need to make our decision for Christ and eternity. Many of the decisions we make have eternal consequences.

Few individuals have actually taken the time to contemplate what it will be like at the second coming of Christ. Note for just a moment that before this event there will be "seven last plagues," the last of which is a great earthquake so strong that nothing that has ever occurred on earth can compare with it (Rev. 16:18). Millions of earth's inhabitants will be killed during these plagues. That's why God's call to His children is "Come out of her [false religious systems], my people, lest you share in her sins, and lest you receive of her plagues" (Rev. 18:4). There are other verses that also indicate that God's people will not receive these plagues, such as Psalm 91:10: "No evil shall befall you, nor shall any plague come near your dwelling."

The wicked who are not destroyed by the plagues will be destroyed "with the brightness of His coming" (2 Thess. 2:8). And since the righteous on earth are in the minority, that means that literally billions of dead bodies will cover the earth as a result of the events of the Second Coming. The Bible says, "And at that day the slain of the Lord shall be from one end of the earth even to the other end of the earth. They shall not be lamented, or gathered, or buried; they shall become refuse on the ground" (Jer. 25:33). The Second Coming will not be a secret. It will be the most significant event to occur on the earth since the Creation.

For some reason people have always wanted to minimize the impact of the Second Coming and somehow put off the day of reckoning, or to lengthen the time of earthly probation. When Jesus was on earth the Pharisees asked Him when the kingdom of God would come. Jesus went to considerable length to make sure they understood that it wouldn't be a secret. This experience is recorded in chapter 17 of Luke's Gospel. Jesus stated in essence that no one will have to tell you that He has come the second time. In fact, He said, if someone says He is over here or over there, don't go see! Then Jesus gave three illustrations to underscore the fact that the Second Coming will be a big event.

The first is a lightning storm, with powerful flashes that go from one end of heaven to the other. The second is the Flood in the time of Noah. Jesus told His listeners, "As it was in the days of Noah, so it will be also in the days of the Son of Man: They ate, they drank, they married wives, they were given in marriage, until the day that Noah entered the ark, and the flood came and destroyed them all" (Luke 17:26, 27). Several factors are evident in this illustration. Apparently life was going on rather normally until suddenly the Flood came and destroyed them all. Eight righteous people—Noah and his family—were saved in the ark, but all the wicked were destroyed at once.

Jesus' third illustration of what it will be like at

His coming is as follows: "Likewise as it was also in the days of Lot: They ate, they drank, they bought, they sold, they planted, they built; but on the day that Lot went out of Sodom it rained fire and brimstone from heaven and destroyed them all. Even so will it be in the day when the Son of Man is revealed" (verses 29, 30). In the stories of Noah and of Lot, life is apparently going on quite normally and then all of a sudden the wicked are all destroyed! Jesus said that this is what it will be like when He comes again. How, then, can we be ready? Apparently, as in the case of the deer on the highway, we must make our decision ahead of time and be ready for this climactic event.

Jesus concluded His warning to the Pharisees with a short, three-word statement: "Remember Lot's wife" (verse 32). What did He mean by this? What should we do about it? Evidently the answer is found in the Old Testament account of Lot and his family. It is certainly worth our review, since the same questions are before us today.

Remember Lot's Wife

The story of Lot and his wife is recorded along with the story of Abram in Genesis 12-19. When God called Abram to leave the city of Ur his nephew Lot accompanied him. God had promised to bless Abram and all the families of the earth through him. And God did indeed bless them. In Genesis 13:2 Abram is described as "very rich in livestock, in silver, and in gold." Lot was also a rich man. In fact, "their possessions were so great that they could not dwell together" (verse 6). Their herders were quarreling about grazing and watering rights.

When Abram heard about the strife he called Lot for a meeting and stated that it was not good for relatives to fight with one another. He suggested that they should separate from each other and asked Lot to choose first from the surrounding countryside. Lot probably should have let Abram have the first choice, since he was the senior man; Lot had been just an associate of Abram. But apparently Lot had his eye on the beautiful Jordan River valley, and so they separated. Some of the saddest words in the Bible are that Lot "pitched his tent toward Sodom" (Gen. 13:12, KJV).

Since the time of the Garden of Eden it has apparently been God's choice for humans that they should lead a more rural or pastoral life rather than pack together in cities. We are to choose country living, not to be exclusive or reclusive, but rather to be able to raise our families away from the stress, noise, violence, pollution, and immorality so prevalent in the cities. To be closer to nature than to the money-crazed society.

The story continues in Genesis 14, with Lot living in Sodom. In the course of time four kings came and made war with the five kings in the Jordan River valley. The four kings prevailed and took all the goods of Sodom and Gomorrah and all their provisions. They also took all the able-bodied people to be their slaves. This slave group included Lot and his family. Word of this conquest came to Abram by someone who had escaped capture. Abram could have said of the situation, "Lot made his bed; let him sleep in it. He chose to live in Sodom. If he had chosen to live up here on the plateau, he would have been safe." But he didn't. Instead he armed his 318 trained servants and pursued the hostile kings. Much as Gideon did years later, Abram divided his men into smaller groups and attacked the kings at night. He was successful in rescuing all the hostages and in recovering all the goods that were taken from Sodom and Gomorrah.

Abram Is Offered the Spoils

The king of Sodom was not among the hostages, because he had hidden himself in a slime pit during the raid. When Abram returned with the people and the goods, the king of Sodom met him. He offered Abram the goods as a reward for the rescue of the hostages and their safe return. But in deference to his covenant with God, Abram declined to take anything for himself. He depended on God to the point that he didn't want any person to say that they had made Abram rich. The offer of the goods to Abram was no small thing. Can you imagine the value of the goods plundered from two prospering cities? Having this amount of stuff would be equivalent to winning the Reader's Digest Sweepstakes, the Virginia Lottery, and the Publishers Clearinghouse Sweepstakes all in one day, plus some!

Apparently Abram knew the principle that where your treasure is, there will your heart be also. And that one cannot serve God and money. Abram was able to say, in essence, "I don't need the money. I depend on God to take care of me." Likely Sarai, Abram's wife, was not present when he declined the goods and money. She could have said, "What do you mean, 'We don't need the money'? We are living in a tent!" But Abram chose to live in a tent to show his family and those around him that he was a pilgrim and a stranger on this earth and that he was waiting "for the city which has foundations, whose builder and maker is God" (see Heb. 11:8-10).

Abram is called by many the father of the faithful. What he did next on that occasion is one of the reasons. He returned a tenth of the spoil to God through Melchizedek, a priest of the God Most High (Gen. 14:18). This is the first mention of tithing in the Bible. But it is mentioned rather casually as a common practice of Abram. Faithful people still tithe today. In so doing they demonstrate their thankfulness to God for His blessing and protection and they show their willingness to trust fully in His provisions.

Moving Back Into Sodom

In spite of what they had just been through, Lot moved his family right back into Sodom! Why don't we ever learn? But the next experience that happened to Lot is why Jesus said, "Remember Lot's wife," so let's move on. This experience also involved Abram and demonstrated God's great mercy and also His judgment. I will give a brief summary of this experience in my own words but you can read all the details in Genesis 18 and 19.

Abraham (his name had been changed by God from Abram to Abraham in Genesis 17) was sitting in the door of his tent one day when he saw three men passing by on the road. He could have just thrown up his hand and waved at them, but instead he jumped up and ran out to greet them. He invited them to stop and rest a while at his place, and offered to wash their tired feet and prepare them a meal. In the process of hosting the three men, Abraham realized that it was God and two angels who were his guests. God announced on this visit that Sarah would have a son.

As God and the angels stood to leave, Abraham went with them a ways to send them on their way. At this point God told the angels to go ahead, that He would stay behind and tell Abraham why they had come. He did this because Abraham was obedient and righteous before Him. God then told Abraham that it had been reported to Him that Sodom and Gomorrah were very wicked. He had come to check it out, and if the reports were true, He would destroy those two cities.

You can imagine what immediately popped into Abraham's mind. *What about Lot and his family?* Then maybe he thought that by now Lot probably had won others to the cause of God, and that surely there were 50 righteous people living in Sodom. So he said to God, "Would You destroy righteous people with the wicked? There might be 50 righteous people down there." Then Abraham made that famous statement, "Far be it from You to do such a thing as this, to slay the righteous with the wicked. . . . Shall not the Judge of all the earth do right?" (Gen. 18:25).

God answered Abraham by saying, "If there are 50 righteous people in Sodom, I will not destroy it for their sakes."

But then Abraham began to wonder if there really

were 50 righteous people in Sodom. He also realized that he was dealing with his Creator. And so he said in effect, "I know that You are the Creator and that I am but dust, but what if there were five fewer than the 50?"

God did the subtraction and responded, "If I find 45 I will not destroy it."

Still concerned about Lot and his family, Abraham asked again, "What if there were only 40 righteous?" And God again responded in the affirmative. To this point in his negotiating with God Abraham had bargained only in increments of five, but now he became bolder on behalf of Lot and asked what if there were only 30, only 20, and finally what if only 10 should be found there. And God responded, "I will not destroy it for the sake of 10."

One of the most fascinating insights we can learn from this experience is that God did not stop granting mercy until Abraham stopped asking! Abraham could likely have saved the city for one person—but he stopped asking! Remember that the Lord wants us to be persistent in our prayers. Genesis 19 begins with the two angels arriving at Sodom in the evening. Apparently they acted as if they were traveling sales-people and prepared to spend the night in the open square in the middle of town. Lot, perhaps because of his position in the city, was sitting in the gate of Sodom. To his credit he still had some of Abraham's hospitality within himself, and he invited the strangers to spend the night in his home. The men expressed re-luctance, but Lot insisted, and so they went with him.

What happened next used to seem incredible, but not so much anymore in today's society. After Lot had fed the strangers supper, but just before they retired for the night, the homosexual men of the city, both old and young, surrounded Lot's house and shouted out to Lot to send the two strangers out to them that they might "sodomize" them. Lot went out to reason with them and discourage them from their sinful intentions, but to no avail. Threatening to harm him, they rushed at him, but the strangers within opened the door, pulled Lot inside, and struck the crowd outside with blindness.

From the biblical perspective this sinful perversion, homosexuality, was the last straw for Sodom, and sealed its doom. The angels revealed themselves as messengers from heaven. They asked Lot, "Have you anyone else here? Sons-in-law, sons, daughters, or whoever you have—take them out of this place, for the Lord has sent us to destroy it."

Lot left his home immediately and went out into the night to warn his married daughters, but they all laughed at him. His daughters were influenced by their husbands. They were well off where they were. They could see no evidence of danger. Everything seemed just fine to them. They had considerable wealth and possessions and could not believe that their beautiful city would be destroyed.

Lot returned home very sorrowful. His wife refused to leave without the kids, and Lot himself felt it was hard to forsake his nice home and all the things he had worked his entire life for. And so they lingered—all night—until the first rays of dawn pierced the sky. Then the angels took Lot and his wife and the two daughters who were still in his house by the hand

and brought them out of the city.

Then something incredible happened. God, who had stayed behind to talk with Abraham, met them as the angels returned to the city for its destruction. God said, "Escape for your life! Do not look behind you nor stay anywhere in the plain. Escape to the mountains, lest you be destroyed" (Gen. 19:17). But though the very Prince of heaven was at his side, Lot expressed fear of the mountains and asked that he be allowed to go to a little nearby town. While he was thus discussing his fate with God, his wife looked back and became a pillar of salt.

She looked back! Why? Apparently because her deliverance meant that she must leave behind her possessions and her children. Instead of thankfully accepting the mercy of God she presumptuously looked back, desiring the life of those who had rejected the divine warning. But, you say, it was only the natural thing to do. I agree. It is also natural to turn the wheel of your car sharply to avoid hitting a deer that jumps out in front of you. But we must decide now what we will do when we are faced with just such a choice as Lot's wife was faced with. What did Jesus mean when He said, "Remember Lot's wife"? Remember, it was in the context of being ready for the Second Coming.

When you "remember" in the biblical sense, it is not just an abstract recollection. It's not just *Oh yes, I remember Lot's wife. Wasn't she the one who became a pillar of salt?* When you remember in the biblical sense you *do* something. When God remembered Hannah she had a child whom she named Samuel.

When you remember the Sabbath you keep it holy. And when you remember Lot's wife you decide right now that nothing—no person or any thing—is worth trading for eternal life. Everyone—yes, even you and I—will have to make that decision before Jesus comes. It won't be long until the test will come.

Just take a moment to review the journey you have made through this book. We now realize that it is critical to choose the right map. That map is the Word of God, the Bible. It is the only standard for truth and the guide that will take us to our heavenly destination. It must be our only source of faith and practice. We understand now that down through time God has been in control and understands the past, the present, and the future. Through the prophets Daniel and John and others He has given prophetic insights regarding the end-times. When we compare these prophecies to our earth's history we recognize that we are surely near the end of the world. The nations have come and gone just as God predicted. The great signs of the end are heralding the coming of Jesus.

And, significantly, the message of hope in the Second Coming is going around the world. Thousands are on the road back to biblical orthodoxy. The biblical Sabbath is being recognized and accepted as men, women, and young people study the Bible for themselves while seeking for truth and meaning for our times. Surely we are almost home.

Everyone who is alive on earth when Jesus returns will have to make a decision similar to that of Lot and his wife. The bottom line is quite simple: Am I prepared to follow the counsel of Jesus through His Word and to leave this earth when He comes, or will I be so tied to people and possessions that I am unwilling to leave them? Jesus said, "He who loves father or mother more than Me is not worthy of Me. And he who loves son or daughter more than Me is not worthy of Me" (Matt. 10:37). I know this sounds radical, but in the end there will be only the saved and the lost. The wicked dead strewn from one end of the earth to the other, and the living righteous on the way to heaven with Jesus. Let's plan to be with Jesus. Remember Lot's wife and keep the steering wheel straight!

It's Time to Decide

Just as surely as the angels of God visited Lot and his family in the ancient city of Sodom with a life-saving warning, so surely has the same living God sent angels to us with the last warning message for humanity. As we have noted from a review of Revelation 14 and 18, the angels are announcing that the hour of God's judgment of the earth has come. It's time to get back to the worship of the Creator God—the one who memorialized His creation with the seventh-day Sabbath. It is time to take stock of our life's journey to determine that we are on the road to the heavenly city. We must reexamine the Word of God and use only it as our map and guide. It's time to leave the false worship that is based on tradition and the teachings of men. God is calling, "Come out of her, My people!" Time is short. We are almost home! Join the thousands who are seeking God's will and way; become a part of the faithful who are taking this final warning to the world!

Experience happiness no problem can take away!

When problems weigh you down, where do you turn? Millions of people have found the answer in a relationship with Jesus Christ.

Happiness Digest shows how you too can experience His joy and guidance, and offers help in the calm assurance that God is in ultimate control and very much interested in your life.

If you enjoyed this book, then you'll want to also read . . .

How to Survive in the 21st Century

Whatever the twenty-first century holds, this book helps you to prepare mentally, physically, emotionally, and spiritually to master its demands. Herbert Douglass explains how to develop the qualities needed to prosper in the coming age: enthusiasm, perseverance, and a winning attitude. He explains how to get out of debt, conquer stress, increase your fitness, solve problems by unleashing your creativity, replace bad habits with good, and plan your destiny. Finally, Douglass takes the long view and reveals how to develop the fortitude to withstand the ultimate crisis of the ages. Paperback, 139 pages. US$2.49, Can$3.69.

A Bridge Across Time

Dan M. Appel weaves a fascinating story about an employee and his boss who discover some surprising things about Sabbathkeeping. Paper, 125 pages. US$2.49, Can$3.59.

The Day Evil Dies

Well-known author Clifford Goldstein provides a behind-the-scenes glimpse into the war between Christ and Satan and helps you understand your role in this great cosmic conflict. Paper, 128 pages. US$1.99, Can$2.99.

Incredible Facts From Your Amazing Bible

Marvin Hunt invites you into the incredible world of the Bible, where mysteries, oddities, and fascinating facts await you. Topics include angels, hell, the mark of the beast, the Sabbath, heaven, the Second Coming, and death. Paperback, 128 pages. US$2.49, Can$3.59.

Project Sunlight

June Strong's gripping story about what it could be like in the final days just before Jesus comes again provides a moving illustration of God's tender concern for His children. Paperback, 128 pages. US$1.99, Can$2.99.

Sixty Ways to Energize Your Life

Here you'll find 60 ways to boost your spiritual, physical, and mental health. Authored by health professionals and inspirational writers, this book will bring you closer to God and help you learn to honor Him through healthy choices. Compiled by Jan W. Kuzma, Kay Kuzma, and DeWitt S. Williams. Paperback, 128 pages. US$2.49, Can$3.69.

Thirteen Life-changing Secrets

Mark Finley, host of the popular TV program *It Is Written,* shares Bible secrets that can make an exciting difference in your life. Discover the peace of forgiveness, the joy of Sabbath rest, the promise of heaven, the power of prayer, and special Bible truths for today. Paper, 122 pages. US$1.99, Can $2.99.

Your Bible and You

Arthur S. Maxwell's popular explanation of Bible truths has been a best-seller for 30 years. His crystal-clear explanations will give you understandings of what the Bible says and its meaning for your life. Paper, 254 pages. US$2.99, Can$4.49.

To order, call 1-800-765-6955.

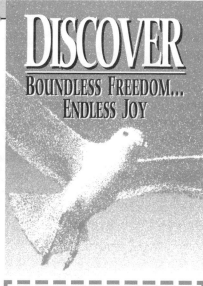